Memoir of a Black Christian Nationalist

SEEDS OF LIBERATION

Shelley McIntosh, EdD

Copyright © 2021 Shelley McIntosh

All rights reserved. No part of this book may be reproduced or transmitted in any form or by any means, electronic or mechanical, including photocopying, recording, or by any information storage and retrieval system, without permission in writing from the author or publisher.

To contact the author for media engagements or for signed copies,
email shelleymcintosh53@gmail.com

Ebook - 978-1-954414-17-4
Hardback - 978-1-954414-18-1
Paperback - 978-1-954414-19-8

Interior design and cover design:
Deborah Perdue: www.illuminationgraphics.com

Editor: Margaret A. Harrell: https://margaretharrell.com

BLB—Berean Literal Bible, © 2016 Berean Bible. Used by Permission. All rights reserved.

ESV—The ESV® Bible (The Holy Bible, English Standard Version®) is adapted from the Revised Standard Version of the Bible, copyright Division of Christian Education of the National Council of the Churches of Christ in the U.S.A. All rights reserved.

KJV—King James Version, public domain.

NASB—New American Standard Bible, Copyright © 1960, 1962, 1963, 1968, 1971, 1972, 1973, 1975, 1977, 1995 by The Lockman Foundation, La Habra, Calif. All rights reserved.

NIV—THE HOLY BIBLE, NEW INTERNATIONAL VERSION®, NIV® Copyright © 1973, 1978, 1984, 2011 by Biblica, Inc.™ Used by permission. All rights reserved worldwide.

NKJV—New King James Version®. Copyright © 1982 by Thomas Nelson. Used by permission. All rights reserved.

RSV—Revised Standard Version of the Bible, copyright © 1946, 1952, and 1971 the Division of Christian Education of the National Council of the Churches of Christ in the United States of America. Used by permission. All rights reserved.

Dedication

Late Reverend Albert B. Cleage Jr. (Jaramogi Abebe Agyeman)
Late Granddaughter, Ni'Jah Monifa
My daughter and son, Lateefah and Italo
Grandsons, Dwight, David, and Italo
Love always . . .

Contents

Acknowledgments vi
Preface vii
I. The Black Messiah 1
II. Black Christian Nationalism 5
III. The Revolutionary Holy Spirit Is Born Anew in Each Generation 11
IV. The Church as Change Agent 31
V. Politics Are Sacred 65
VI. Building Counterinstitutions 69
VII. Communalism—Reflection of Man's Higher Nature 111
VIII. The Experience of God 119
IX. The Community of Jesus 133
X. Appendices 143
    Appendix A—BCN Message and Mission 144
    Appendix B—Poetry by Jaramogi 164
    Appendix C—BCN Covenant 187
    Appendix D—BCN Statement of Faith 188
    Appendix E—BCN Code 190
    Appendix F—BCN Program 195
    Appendix G—BCN Teaches 197
    Appendix H—BCN Position 199
    Appendix I—BCN Goals at Basic Training Levels 200
    Appendix J—BCN Basic Training Pledge 203
References 205
About the Author 207

Acknowledgments

A special gratitude to all who struggled together, whether it was five years or thirty years. Your names are eternalized, and your works will soar in this great universe as expansive energy touching the present and the future. Feel enamored that we became a people who came out of Detroit.

To Sondai Lester and Lindiwe Lester, you are my examples of great leadership. Dr. Diane Fabu Jackson, your spiritual insight and impactful coaching sharpened my perception and self-awareness.

Publishing a book is not done alone. Thank you, Deborah Perdue of Illumination Graphics for the amazing interior and cover designs. Heartfelt appreciation to Joni Wilson for thorough and expert editing. My indebtedness to Elizabeth Atkins of Two Sisters Writing and Publishing for the redirection of my manuscript and for offering details in storytelling. To Jackie Smith of J. Merrill Publishing, much gratitude for your passion and professionalism. Because of all of you, thoughts became written words, and written words birthed a book. I am eternally grateful.

Preface

FOURTEEN HUNDRED BUILDINGS, RED ORANGE FLAMES BILLOWING toward the sky, smoldering debris, now broken and leveled, smoke settling in an eerie pall, bullets piercing the air and finding a resting place in the flesh of forty-three Black bodies, harassment by police, and occupation by 7,000 National Guard and United States Army troops; Detroit was a city rebelling against injustice in 1967. From the time Cadillac brought the first slave to Detroit in 1701 to plant crops and construct buildings to the tumultuous 1960s and 1970s, Black people were subjugated by a brutal racist oppressive system. Their anger reached a climax.

Unequal housing laws crammed about 60,000 people into 460 acres in the Virginia Park neighborhood. Most lived in tiny, subdivided apartments. The Detroit Police Department was viewed as a White occupying army.

The entire city was in a state of economic and social strife: Automobile companies moved to outsourcing and technology. Thousands of unskilled Black men were permanently laid off, left with no income. Hundreds of thousands of the middle class, both Black and White, left the city by means of newly constructed freeways. These events further gutted Detroit's vitality and left behind vacant storefronts, widespread unemployment, and impoverished despair.

Detroit was one of the many metropolitan areas across the US where White flight dramatically reduced the tax base of formerly prosperous cities. The flight caused urban blight, poverty, and racial discord.

"Stop the Robberies, Enjoy Safe Streets," known as STRESS, was a Detroit Police Department unit; its purpose was to reduce the crime in Detroit. In operation from 1971 until 1974, black unmarked police cars carrying four police officers, The Big Four, targeted African American men. In rapid speed, riding up on the Black men, braking to a screeching halt, all four jumping out of the police car, surrounding the suspect, and brutally handcuffing him in full view of children and the elderly was intimidating and threatening. STRESS led to the deaths of twenty-four men, twenty-two of them African American, over the course of three-and-a-half years.

Birth of the Shrines of the Black Madonna

It is out of this Black experience of racism and injustice that Reverend Albert B. Cleage Jr. (Jaramogi Abebe Agyeman) founded the Shrines of the Black Madonna. His ideals were shaped by his parents, Pearl D. Cleage and Dr. Albert B. Cleage Sr. Both were catalysts for his activism. Pearl D. Cleage was a founder of St. John's Presbyterian Church and the Shrine of the Black Madonna in Detroit. She often lectured on African American history and was a member of the auxiliaries of the Iota Boule and Alpha Phi Alpha fraternities. She organized the West Side Human Relations Council in the 1930s.

Dr. Albert B. Cleage Sr. practiced medicine for forty-two years in the city of Detroit, sixteen of which he served on the staff at Receiving Hospital. He was a graduate of Knoxville College and the University of Indiana Medical School and a member of the Alpha Phi Alpha and Iota Boule chapter of the Sigma Pi Phi fraternities. Extremely active in the political and cultural life of Detroit, he was a charter member of Central Congregational Church, one of its most ardent financial supporters.

Dr. Cleage helped found Dunbar Hospital, Detroit's only hospital that granted admitting privileges to Black doctors and trained African American residents. Dr. Cleage was a major figure in the Detroit medical community, even being designated as city physician by Mayor Charles Bowles in 1930. The stark awareness of Black reality began with his parents, and it became sharper as he witnessed and participated in the civil rights movement.

A Black Christian Activist

Reverend Cleage was a Christian activist. After being involved in the civil rights movement and forming friendships with leaders such as Reverend Martin L. King Jr., the Honorable Elijah Muhammed, Malcolm X, Stokely Carmichael, historians, and politicians; after publicly debating about the crisis of Black people; after speaking at numerous universities and colleges, Reverend Cleage analyzed that the only way to liberate

Black people is to ground their beliefs in the historical truth about Jesus, thus making Christianity relevant to the Black man's struggle for liberation.

In 1967, he founded the Shrines of the Black Madonna of the Black Christian Nationalist Movement located at 7625 Linwood in Detroit, Michigan. It was later renamed the Shrines of the Black Madonna of the Pan African Orthodox Christian Church. This movement was to encourage Black churches to correctly interpret Jesus' teachings as a means to meet the social, economic, and political needs of Black people. Because of his disciplined study and affiliation with Black historians, Reverend Cleage discovered that Jesus was a Black man born of a Black mother. Her name, Mary.

In the church, Reverend Cleage installed a sixteen-foot painting of the Black Madonna Mary holding her baby Jesus, the Black Messiah. This was a strong and controversial religious statement that honored the important role of Black women. It also was a profound attempt to correct an insidious untruth about the race and life of Jesus. Indeed, Jesus was a Black Messiah born of a Black mother during the time that Israel was oppressed and persecuted by the Romans.

Reverend Cleage wrote about this in his book, *The Black Messiah*. The struggles of Israel coincide with Black people's struggle today and with the Black Lives Matter movement; all fighting against racism and oppression.

The Seeds of Liberation

This is my story of being a member of the Black Christian Nationalist (BCN) Movement in the years from 1971 to 2000. I interweave the historical phases of the church's evolution within a tapestry of my personal experiences. It is a blending of technical and creative writing done with the intent to share informatively and experientially. I intertwine my memories throughout the book to paint the canvas of how the written program is married to actual human events.

Service under the Leadership of Reverend Cleage

I served under the leadership of Reverend Cleage for thirty years, being one of those thousands of young Black people who joined the Shrines of the Black Madonna in the

1970s. Because of his constant teachings and total commitment to bring into being a self-sufficient Nation, I was one of those who experienced and witnessed him face to face. Rising through the ranks of leadership as a minister, bishop, and cardinal, I sat in his presence numerous times while learning and evolving.

    I served as a group leader to children and adult groups. I preached sermons and lectured Black theology classes, taught the spiritual disciplines of yoga and meditation, and developed the children's institute named Mtoto House, which was designed to support the spiritual, social, academic, and physical growth of children. I christened babies and performed marriages. I worked beside Reverend Cleage to develop KUA, the science of becoming what you already are. Being totally committed to the work of the church, I am one of the living witnesses of what it is like to be a Black Christian Nationalist.

I

The Black Messiah

JESUS WAS BORN TO A BLACK MADONNA. HER NAME WAS MARY.

Over the past twenty years, extensive DNA research has been conducted on the Jewish people. Studies were first done with Caucasian Jews. The DNA results indicate that Jews have a common genetic makeup, specifically a Y-chromosome haplotype that is passed down through the mother.

African Jews, who have always identified themselves as such, desired that their DNA be tested. The same Y-chromosome haplotype was found, except it was denser, linking them more directly with Judaism. Today, Jews can be identified by their common genealogy.

The Lemba Jews of Zimbabwe and the Igbo Jews of Nigeria also have this genetic makeup. They have always claimed that they are Jews. Currently, studies are being conducted on the biblical ten lost tribes of Israel, which the Lemba and the Igbo people may belong to. Historically, the ten tribes were exiled by the Assyrians, which has stirred discussions linking the US slave trade with the diaspora of millions of African Jews across the world. The original chosen people of God are Africans, whereas, European Jews are converts to Judaism. This certainly is unsettling to millions of people. Nevertheless, DNA testing is uncovering historical truth (Tamarkin).

The genealogy of Jesus is found in Matthew 1:1–17 (NIV). Verses 12–17 read as follows.

After the exile to Babylon:
Jeconiah was the father of Shealtiel,
Shealtiel the father of Zerubbabel,
Zerubbabel the father of Abihud,

> *Abihud the father of Eliakim,*
> *Eliakim the father of Azor,*
> *Azor the father of Zadok,*
> *Zadok the father of Akim,*
> *Akim the father of Elihud,*
> *Elihud the father of Eleazar,*
> *Eleazar the father of Matthan,*
> *Matthan the father of Jacob,*
> *and Jacob the father of Joseph, the husband of Mary, and Mary was the mother of Jesus who is called the Messiah.*
> *Thus there were fourteen generations in all from Abraham to David, fourteen from David to the exile to Babylon, and fourteen from the exile to the Messiah.*

Logically, because Jesus is a descendant of Abraham historically and genetically, Jesus was Black. He was the Messiah, the liberator, who would deliver the Jewish people from Roman oppression. The genetic connection is evidence of who he was. As important is the proof of today's Ethiopians who are Jews and can trace their genealogy to King Solomon.

Christianity is an outgrowth of the Jewish religion based on the belief of the risen Christ and the gospel spread by Jesus' disciples after Pentecost. As Rome was declining, the commitment and revolutionary passion of the early Christians served as motivation for Rome to convert to Christianity, specifically done with the hope that it could rebuild its empire.

Many of the Christian tenets believed and practiced today are based on misinterpretations and modifications by Roman cardinals and bishops. These can be found in the Council of Nicaea sessions. Decisions about the date to celebrate Jesus' birth, as well as defining him as God through the concept of the Holy Trinity were debated and decided on in these meetings. Over time, the interpretation of Jesus' life was taken out of context. Instead of his revolutionary nature being portrayed as significant, his death to save all humankind overshadowed it.

Jesus, born of a Black Madonna, makes Christianity a Black man's religion relevant to the Black man's struggle for liberation in today's world. Reverend Cleage discussed this in detail in his book, *The Black Messiah*, first published in 1968.

II

Black Christian Nationalism

REVEREND CLEAGE WAS A CHRISTIAN, A BLACK CHRISTIAN, A DEVOUT believer in Jesus. His mission was to bring Black Christians back to a more conscious understanding of their African history in order to effect positive progression as a whole; in essence, to build a Nation within a Nation with power.

A nation is a cultural-political community that is conscious of its autonomy, unity, and particular interests, potentially growing into a form of nationalism. Reverend Cleage further defined a nation as a group of people united to obtain or perpetuate their power. It is self-governing with the capacity to touch the lives of its people. Its goal is to create institutions that serve the welfare of the people. It ensures that basic needs of food, shelter, and clothing are met. It assumes the responsibilities of providing health services, education, protection, and opportunities. It supports the psychological human needs of health, happiness, and prosperity.

A nation with power explicitly means to have control over the institutional structure that governs a group's life. Reverend Cleage's position was that Black people are separated. Upon this systematic separation, we live within the US but are powerless. In light of this reality, Black people must be unified by laws, practices, and policies that ensure their welfare and survival; a Black Nation with power that peacefully coexists with other nations.

He discussed the new directions for the Black church in his book, *Black Christian Nationalism: New Directions for the Black Church,* first published in 1972. He wrote the following.

> *"At the Shrine of the Black Madonna, we recognize and admit the betrayal of the Black Church even as we struggle to redeem and transform it for the survival struggle which lies ahead. If the Black Church is to commit its resources to the Black revolution, we must develop a new Black Theology founded upon a critical re-examination of the historic foundation of the Christian faith. We know that the Israel of the Old Testament period was a Black Nation. We know that Mary and Joseph and Jesus were Black. So, Christianity is founded upon the life and teachings of a Black Messiah.*
>
> *As important as the fact that Israel and Jesus were Black, is the fact that Jesus was a revolutionary leader engaged in a liberation struggle against the white gentile world. In light of these facts, the meaning of the Bible is dramatically changed and Christianity is a Black man's religion, relevant to the Black Revolution. The Black Church must build upon this foundation.*
>
> *Shrines of the Black Madonna seek to bring the Black Church back to its historic roots through the Black Christian Nationalist Church established in March of 1967."*

The purpose of the Shrines of the Black Madonna coincides with the teachings of Jesus and what he believed God called him to do. Jesus' message was the same message of the Prophet Isaiah found in the Old Testament.

> *"The Spirit of the Sovereign LORD is on me, because the LORD has anointed me to preach good news to the poor. He has sent me to bind up the brokenhearted, to proclaim freedom for the captives and release from darkness for the prisoners, to proclaim the year of the LORD's favor and the day of vengeance of our God, to comfort all who mourn"* (Isaiah 61:1–2, NIV).
>
> In Luke 4:18–19, NIV, Jesus said, *"The Spirit of the Lord is on me, because he has anointed me to proclaim good news to the poor. He has sent me to proclaim freedom for the prisoners and recovery of sight for the blind, to set the oppressed free, to proclaim the year of the Lord's favor!"*

Liberty is the state of being free within society from oppressive restrictions imposed by authority on a group of people's ways of life and their sovereignty. The oppressed are the downtrodden whose lives have been diminished and threatened by a brutally powerful racist system.

The Spirit of the Lord has been given to each of us by birthright. So, the Black church can be the institution that unifies the skills, talents, and gifts of millions of African Americans, African descendants abroad, and Africans on the continent of Africa. It can become that force to set the downtrodden free, to build institutions that serve Black people, and to create economic and political power.

Reverend Cleage undertook the important task of restructuring the theology and program of the Shrines of the Black Madonna. Having made a decision to cease public presentations and debates, his attention and intention were to build a movement with young people. The discussions in *Black Christian Nationalism, New Directions for the Black Church* were operationalized in the Shrines of the Black Madonna. With his life dedicated to the inner work of building a nation, Reverend Cleage developed a comprehensive program that was put into action by members. As he often said, *"Nation building is more than just a notion."*

Oppression Still Exists

Today, Black people are still oppressed. Lynchings still occur through the institutions of police organizations and mobs of renegades as well as organized White supremacist groups. Laws are still created with the intent to suppress Black voting power and upward mobility. Educational institutions are ill-equipped to teach the basic skills of reading, writing, and mathematics, leaving Black children with fewer opportunities for academic achievement and improved quality of life.

Close to forty million people live in poverty in the United States. Thirty-five million are food insecure, which is simply a fancy term for hunger. Black people currently make up about 13.8 percent of the US population, and about 27 percent fall below the poverty line. The poverty population overall rates at about 15 percent. So Black people in the United States face nearly twice the risk of being impoverished as average Americans.

Black men are especially likely to be imprisoned. Among those ages twenty-five to twenty-nine, one-in-twenty Black men were in state or federal prison in 2018. Black people make up 12 percent of the population, while 33 percent are imprisoned. These statistics are higher than any other group in the US.

As a light is being shone on police brutality and racial injustice, Americans also need to recognize and address the injustice that takes place every day in our classrooms. On national tests in 2020, only 18 percent of Black fourth graders scored proficient or above in reading as compared to 45 percent of White fourth graders. Black eighth graders scored 15 percent compared to 42 percent of White eighth graders.

Our reality is the same as it was in the 1970s. Discrimination, racism, oppression, and exploitation are embedded in laws and policies enforceable by court systems, the police, and the military. These laws include housing discrimination, gentrification, biased healthcare, unfair employment, prejudicial taxation, minimum wages, and racial incarceration.

We are systematically limited to building wealth as a people globally and locally. For example, Africa is not represented in the G7, the Group of Seven, an intergovernmental political forum consisting of Canada, France, Germany, Italy, Japan, the United Kingdom, and the United States. Its purpose is to discuss and act in concert to help resolve problems, with a special focus on economic issues. They represent more than 62 percent of the global net wealth. Although Africa is not included, the wealth of each country in the G7 depends on Africa's resources.

Along the same lines, another example is the National Collegiate Athletic Association (NCAA). It is a membership organization of colleges and universities whose fundamental charge is to maintain intercollegiate athletics as an integral part of the educational program and the athlete as an integral part of the student body. Approximately 1,050 colleges and universities and a number of other affiliates are members. About 360,000 students participate in intercollegiate athletics at these member institutions each year.

Black men comprise 57–70 percent of college football players. While the NCAA generates over $531 billion in football alone, the players do not share the wealth. Yet, the monetary success of the NCAA depends on Black players' performance. The G7 and the NCAA are both examples of creating wealth for specific countries and individuals. This is done at the expense of exploitation. Wealth is created by policies and so is poverty.

Within the midst of systematic oppression, the mindset of a significant number of people of all races is based on selfishness and greed. Without the awareness that each human being is connected, and that each person has value because of his or her miraculous birth, people feel alienated. Not only from others, but they also feel alienated from themselves. Many are unaware that they are connected to the Source that gives and permeates all life.

The illusion of separation is the outcome of a capitalistic world system that values profit over people and that rapes the earth of its resources. The world system created by powerful nations is not aligned with the harmonious, balanced, and abundant nature of God. This disconnection and misalignment make it easy for people to prey on others, to abuse, and to murder. There is Black-on-Black crime as well as White-on-White crime. Both are destructive and diabolical. Conquering other countries and settling individual conflicts are both accomplished with artillery that terminate precious human lives, including children.

"The world is in bondage to sin," Jaramogi proclaimed.

The state of Black people in this world is still one of disparity. Although the media focuses on the wealth of a handful of Black people, the median wealth for Black families is $17,000 as compared to $171,000 for Whites. Moreover, higher numbers have been elected to political offices, serve as attorney generals, university professors, police chiefs, mayors, chief executive officers, and even president and vice-president of the United States. Our challenge is building united power so that all can be free of oppression, injustice, poverty, miseducation, and police brutality. When one Black person is oppressed, we are all oppressed. Certainly, this is the type of identification, a mindset, so urgently needed now.

The institution of the Black church must no longer separate us because of different tenets, protocols, and beliefs. There is one on almost every street block. Oftentimes situated in a blighted neighborhood, it has no power to rebuild its desecrated surroundings. The Black church can be more relevant to uniting all the resources, talents, skills, and monies of its congregations to build power; however, a lack of an overarching theological belief poses an obstacle. It is time to unite under the banner of Jesus.

> *"The Spirit of the Lord is on me, because he has anointed me to proclaim good news to the poor. He has sent me to proclaim freedom for the prisoners and recovery of sight for the blind, to set the oppressed free"* (Luke 4:18, NIV).

III

The Revolutionary Holy Spirit Is Born Anew in Each Generation

I WAS BORN ON EARTH ON NOVEMBER 20, 1949, AT 2:45 A.M. I LEFT MY mother's internal womb to be welcomed by the greater nurturer, Mother Earth. My parents decided to name me Shelley Elaine Miller.

Reverend Albert B. Cleage Jr., made his arrival on earth on June 13, 1911. Thirty-eight years separated my arrival from his. Yet, our paths crossed twenty-one years after my birth and sixty years after his.

We Are Energy Beings

Being born into physical existence is a miracle in itself. When I think about life, I am aware that before November 20, 1949, I was not present on earth. In the same light, I am aware that I will disappear at death. I know that each individual is created by two small cells, the female egg and the male sperm that unite to create life. I am keenly aware that this process of rapid cell division within the mother's womb creates major organs, tissues, bones, and blood not commanded by human manipulation but is magnificently orchestrated by a higher intelligence and powerful force that we cannot see. Yet, it is the Source of all creation and known by many names, the Holy Spirit, God, Allah, Jehovah, the Great Spirit, the Unified Energy Field.

This energy undergirds all of life and is present within each of us, the God within, the Inner Divinity. It moves. Out of it springs forth creativity, joy, activity, physical athleticism, wisdom, love, and power. Unblocked, it unveils unlimited potential. Blocked, it renders us blind to the power given to us by birthright.

Being aware of who we really are, God's children, drives us to reach our highest potential, to be free both physically and spiritually. Any act that blocks the movement of inner power, including unjust laws, oppression, relegation to poverty, and human alienation are sins against God, the unifying force of all creation.

Born to Rufus and Ruth Miller

Both of my parents moved from Alabama to Michigan in 1949 during the last Black Migration. My father Rufus James Miller Senior served in World War II as an Army sergeant. After being honorably discharged, he landed a job at Chrysler where he stayed for thirty-three years. For thirty of those years, he was a Baptist pastor who founded the Greater Love Missionary Baptist Church.

He was six feet, two inches, brown skinned, and weighed 245 pounds. How did I know? He told my siblings and me so many times. I believe he knew that he was a good-looking Black man. Because he took so much pride in being an example of a Baptist Christian pastor, he kept tight reins on us.

"God forbids secular music, dancing, and fornication. And so do I."

I never heard a profane word from my father. I never saw him drink or dance.

Being able to provide for his family gave him a sense of power and esteem. He boasted about working at Chrysler, especially when he would get paid time-and-a-half or double-time for overtime. Instead of earning $20 per hour, his pay was $40 an hour. He bought the best of shoes, suits, ties, shirts, and hats that were perfectly contrasted and coordinated. Gathering my two sisters and me, he took us to Crowley's in downtown Detroit, proudly marched in with us in tow, and announced to the saleswoman, "Pick out some dresses for my girls, three apiece." By all means, he was a proud man.

My mother, Ruth Lee Miller, worked briefly as a schoolteacher in the south. In the north, she was a stay-at-home mother who tediously took care of her four children, Vernice, Jacqueline, Rufus James Jr., and me, Shelley Elaine. We were always clean, hair combed, well-fed, and protected. My mother had a fighting spirit protecting her children like an eagle protects its nest.

III – The Revolutionary Holy Spirit Is Born Anew in Each Generation

When she knew that a neighbor placed broken glass between her front yard and ours as a barrier to keep us out of her yard, my mother picked up a two-by-four plank to bash her. The police were called. The situation was settled but not before my mother made it very clear that she would protect her children by any means necessary. We were her pride and joy.

She stood at five feet, two inches, with long, black, thick hair. Chocolate skinned with beautifully sculpted fingers that could sweep up ten jacks in less than a second. She taught us to play jacks, checkers, Chinese checkers, Monopoly, root the peg, and bat and ball. While my mother was more playful, my father was more serious. My siblings and I reaped the benefits of both. Our house was organized and neat.

Both parents taught us through explanation and demonstration. My father taught me how to wash clothes. Taking me into the basement when I was thirteen years old, he separated the dark clothes from the light clothes, filled the washing machine with hot water, prepared two rinse sinks, ran the clothes through the wringer, and then showed me how to hang them up on a clothesline. All the time, he was talking.

"Shelley, this is how you separate the clothes."

"Watch your hands as you put the clothes through the wringer."

"You must have a warm rinse sink, and a cold rinse sink for the clothes."

My mother taught me how to iron. She followed the same method as my father. Showing me how to place a shirt on the ironing board, to iron the collar first, then the back of the shirt, the sleeves and the front followed.

"Shelley, lay the shirt on the ironing board this way."

"Fold the sleeves right here so that it will make a nice crease."

"Now, take care to iron the back so that the iron touches all the material."

One day, when I was nine years old, I lay in bed with my mommy.

"Momma, can you teach me how to braid?" I asked.

She sectioned three parts of her hair.

"This is how you do it. You must have three parts. Cross the left part over the middle section. Now, cross the right part over. Cross the middle part over."

After using her own hair to show me, then she let me practice on her hair. I learned to braid hair in ten minutes.

"Momma, can you teach me to French braid now?"

It was called French braid in the 1950s and 1960s, but its origin is African and is called cornrow braiding. It dates back to 3000 BC, particularly in Ethiopia.

She spoke while at the same time cornrow braiding her own hair.

"Now, you try," she said.

"That was underhand cornrow."

"Look how I do it overhand, Shelley," she continued.

I practiced on my mother's head and learned that day to braid and cornrow.

When we approached teenage years, she started some domestic work in Grosse Pointe, Michigan. I was about twelve years old at the time. One day she took me with her. We rode the bus to Grosse Pointe, walked down a street of manicured lawns and brick houses. Stepping on the pathway leading to the door, I was amazed at the huge size of the house. Upon entering, my mother introduced me to the White family—husband, wife, and three children. One girl seemed to be about my age.

My mother instructed me to clean the stove and to mop the kitchen. She kept a supervisory eye on me as she dusted, wiped baseboards, and washed dishes. After about three hours of cleaning, we were through.

On the way home, I walked by her side wondering what we had just done.

"Momma, why do we have to clean their house when we have a house of our own?" I asked.

She didn't answer. Little did I know then that as smart as my mother was, an unjust society relegated her to be the "help," the domestic worker. She never took me to do domestic work again. Eventually, she became a cook at Howard Johnson's in downtown Detroit.

My mother told me that as a child, I was quiet, timid, and shy. In my quietness, I became aware of the flow of human activity, which seemed magical to me. I had few words to explain this experience as a youngster. However, as an adult, I realized that I was born with a sensitivity to spiritual energies.

Spirituality

I had a dream come true when I was eleven years old. That dream. That dream. It happened when my family and I lived on the east side of Detroit, on Fisher Street to be exact, a block east of Indian Village where beautiful immense houses loomed. Only separated by an alley, my neighborhood stood in stark contrast with our small wooden-framed residences ranging in colors from white to brown to red.

Children played freely on the sidewalks, while attentive adults watched carefully from the porch or through window blinds. Everyone knew one another. A young, handsome guy, about nineteen years old, stayed across the street from my house. He worked on cars and was very friendly. Sometimes, he would play ball with us, just throwing it back and forth, catching, throwing, and catching. One night I dreamed.

I dreamed he had a basketball.

"Whoever catches the ball is my girlfriend," he teased while tossing the basketball into the air.

In the dream, I caught the ball. The next day, it happened just as I dreamed it.

Although I was too young to be anyone's girlfriend, just the sheer youthful joy of it was enough for me. I told no one I had a dream that came true until years later. My next experience was not a dream. It occurred in broad daylight.

I carefully spread out an ivory-colored blanket on the soft, lush, green grass at Belle Isle Park in Detroit, Michigan, preparing a space for my boyfriend and me to lay down. Both of us just nineteen years old bathed in young magical love. He, a handsome dark-skinned man with a thick moustache and in the Air Force. I, a college freshman, caramel-colored petite woman with black, shoulder-length hair. We lay on our backs making small talk.

As I gazed into the serenely beautiful blue sky speckled with white, puffy clouds, something extraordinary happened to me. My boyfriend seemed to disappear into a mirage of consciousness. Unaware of my physical body, I now was emerged, embraced, and encompassed by the sky, the clouds, the birds, the trees in a oneness I experienced so profoundly. It was as if I was in a dream or maybe a trance. I was not in either one.

It could be described as a high, a connection, a communion with everything. I didn't know it then, but I had attained a higher level of consciousness. Feeling dazed, I experienced this state of consciousness for about two hours. I told no one. Was this my first profound God experience? Did these spiritual experiences direct me to my future that I could not yet see? Were they glimpses into who I really am? Was the Spirit of God moving in me?

Connections to the Life of Jesus

The teachings of Jesus, the Black Messiah, and Reverend Albert B. Cleage Jr. reflect a higher consciousness of our existence. Merely observing the physical or three-dimensional world without knowing that the invisible world has a greater impact, our perception of who we really are stays stagnant. Knowledge of our own power remains subdued. Belief in only an external God rather than One that resides in us also keeps us immature to the point that we alienate people.

Instead of being aware that we are all connected, we perpetuate destructiveness through lying, greed, racism, and murders. Humankind has created a world that is in bondage to sin because most people function on the level of individualism, the lowest nature of human beings. In this mindset, people are devalued, giving rise to oppression, racism, injustice, wars, and corruption in government and religious places.

Jesus attempted to raise the consciousness of his people, empowering them to change and to liberate themselves from Roman oppression. In the same light, Reverend Cleage taught that it is important for us to be aware and to know that God Power resides in each of us. It is the basis for transformation, the basis for ending oppression, and the basis for the quest of health, happiness, and prosperity.

"The kingdom of God does not come with observation; nor will they say, 'See here!' or 'See there!' For indeed, the kingdom of God is within you" (Luke 17:20–21, NKJV).

Reverend Cleage said, *"For us the experience of God is the basis of a revolutionary struggle for self-actualization and social change designed to transform our wretched Black condition here on earth."*

The BCN Manifesto of 1969, written by Reverend Cleage, explains even further Black people's reality and what must be done.

> *"We seek to change society to accomplish the liberation of Black people, and we realize that we are engaged in a struggle for power and for survival. We believe that nothing is more sacred than the liberation of Black people. We must transform the minds of Black people, freeing them from dependence upon white cultural values and the unconscious acceptance of the white man's declaration of Black inferiority. We must restructure our relationships*

within the Black Nation in terms of unity and love in preparation for a realistic power struggle against our oppressors. We must control all of the big institutions that dominate the Black community. Self-determination and community control must become realities in every area of ghetto life.

The officers and members of the Shrines of the Black Madonna believe that the Black church can become relevant to the Black revolution. Upon the foundation of this faith, we have undertaken to build a Black Nation within a nation following the teachings of the Black Messiah, Jesus of Nazareth. We realize that society has segregated us and upon this separation we are convinced that we need not be poor, disadvantaged, and exploited if we will but use our separation as a power base for political and economic self-determination rather than permitting it to be used as an instrument and symbol of our enslavement. The Black church must free the minds of Black people from psychological identification with a white society that seeks in every way to destroy them. The Black church must fight to free the Black man's mind so that he can fight to restructure the institutions which perpetuate his enslavement."

Joining the Shrines of the Black Madonna

I was twenty-one years old in 1971 and still living with my parents on Freeland Street located on the west side of Detroit. My three siblings were still there also.

One day, my oldest sister Vernice came home with a bag in hand.

"Look, Shelley. See what I bought."

She pulled out some beautiful blue earrings and a silver bangle. Finally, she took out a book.

It was *The Black Messiah* written by Reverend Albert B. Cleage Jr.

"Vernice, can I read that?" I extended my hand to grab the book.

"Where did you get it?"

"I got it from the Shrine of the Black Madonna Cultural Center and Bookstore. Yes, you can read it, but know where you got it from," she reminded me.

"Okay, okay."

I read the book from cover to cover in a matter of three days.

"Vernice, we've got to visit that church on Sunday."

"Yeah, let's do that. Virginia, our friend, can come with us too."

On that Sunday in January, Vernice, Virginia, and I crunched through snow in the heart of winter. We caught the Fenkell bus, then transferred to the Linwood bus.

We finally arrived at Linwood and Hogarth and entered the brown brick church with its white steeple pointed toward the sky. As we walked through the doors, my eyes were immediately drawn to the huge portrait of the Black Madonna as she seemed to look out over the congregation with pride.

Ushers directed us to available spaces in the pews. The church's capacity is approximately 800 and it overflowed with young African Americans seated both on the main floor and the balcony. The energy level was so high that it seemed to engulf and swish me into its vortex. We made it to our seats as the choir was ending "The Black National Anthem," directed by one of the founders, Oscar Hands. This was followed by the recital of the "Prayer of the Black Messiah," written and led by another founder, Tommy Williams.

Together we prayed.

> *"Almighty God, who called together the Black Nation Israel through Thy Son, the Revolutionary Black Messiah Jesus, hallowed be Thy name. May Thy Black Nation speedily come and Thy will be done on earth as we accept commitment to daily sacrifice and struggle. Give us this day our daily bread. And forgive us our trespasses as we forgive Black brothers and sisters who trespass against us. Help us to resist temptation as we struggle against individualism and may the Black Nation stand as a living witness to Thy power and Thy glory forever and ever. Amen."*

I saw Reverend Cleage for the first time. He was very light skinned and about five feet ten, dressed in a navy-blue suit, a white shirt, and a black bow tie. As he preached, I was captivated. The message was clarified in an intellectual yet powerful delivery about the oppression of Black people. The historical truth about the life and mission of Jesus, the Black Messiah, was exhorted authoritatively. A vivid explanation about the struggles of the

Black Nation Israel compared to the present struggle of Black people was given.

My soul was on fire! The Holy Spirit stirred within me! Then, the invitational call to join was given.

"If you want to become a member of this church, now is the time," Reverend Cleage announced. "If you want to commit yourself to the liberation struggle of Black people, then this church is for you."

The choir began to sing, *"Lead me. Guide me along the way. For if you lead me, I will not stray, Lord, let me walk each day with Thee. Lead me, O, Lord, lead me."*

I turned to my sister excitedly.

"I want to join."

She nodded at me in agreement. The three of us walked down the center aisle, passing cherry wood pews filled with people singing and clapping their hands. We walked past stained-glass windows as each step took us closer to the mural of the Black Madonna. Finally arriving at the front of the pulpit, I shook hands with Reverend Cleage. On that Sunday, seventy joined! The new applicants lined the entire width at the front of the church and wrapped around the left and right aisles.

The Spirit of God had touched me again. I had become a Black Christian Nationalist. Now, the BCN Creed, written by Reverend Cleage, expressed my new beliefs. We were required to memorize it and to recite it at the beginning of each group meeting and at church service.

The Black Christian Nationalist Creed

"I believe that human society stands under the judgment of one God revealed to all and known by many names. His creative power is visible in the mysteries of the universe, in the revolutionary Holy Spirit which will not long permit men to endure injustice nor to wear the shackles of bondage, in the rage of the powerless when they struggle to be free and, in the violence, and conflict which even now threaten to level the hills and the mountains.

I believe that Jesus, the Black Messiah, was a revolutionary leader sent by God to rebuild the Black Nation Israel and to liberate Black people from powerlessness, and from the oppression, brutality and exploitation of the white gentile world.

I believe that the revolutionary Spirit of God embodied in the Black Messiah is born anew in each generation and that Black Christian Nationalists constitute the living remnant of God's chosen people in this day and are charged by him with responsibility for the liberation of Black people.

I believe that both my survival and my salvation depend upon my willingness to reject individualism and so I commit my life to the liberation struggle of Black people and accept the values, ethics, morals and program of the Black Nation defined by that struggle and taught by the Black Christian Nationalist Movement."

Connections to the Life of Jesus

"As Jesus was walking beside the Sea of Galilee, he saw two brothers, Simon called Peter and his brother Andrew. They were casting a net into the lake, for they were fishermen. 'Come, follow me,' Jesus said, 'and I will send you out to fish for people.' At once they left their nets and followed him" (Matthew 4:18–20, NIV).

Jesus lived during the time of apocalyptic nationalism. This is a faith that God would intervene in the affairs of the Black Nation Israel empowering them to be free of Roman oppression. There would be a final battle between the forces of Darkness and the forces of Light, and Israel would live as a sovereign nation, as God's people, a people of the Covenant.

The era of apocalyptic nationalism would be signified by the arrival of a Messiah as taught by the Essene community who set themselves apart from the general population. Their purpose was to live a righteous life, one that was in compliance with the Covenant requirements. In doing so, they would be worthy of God's intervention to usher in a new kingdom.

Hugh J. Schonfield, a scholar of the Dead Sea Scrolls, examined the impact of the Essene community on the life and mission of Jesus. In his 1984 book, *The Essene Odyssey: The Mystery of the True Teacher and the Essene Impact on the Shaping of Human Destiny* (Schonfield, 60), he wrote, *"So strong were the Essene teachings about the End-Time personalities that they were seen to find fulfillment not only in John the Baptist and Jesus, on the side of the forces of Light, but also especially in Jacob (James) son of Joseph and a younger brother of Jesus."*

Jesus was fulfilling the requirements of his messianic calling. When he told Simon and Peter to drop their nets, he was calling them into a revolutionary movement. He was building his inner core of leadership.

Like Jesus, Reverend Cleage called people to join a movement founded on the life and teachings of Jesus, the Black Messiah. In the BCN Statement of Faith, he wrote the following.

> *"We share the faith of Jesus of Nazareth. We embody the revolutionary power of God revealed in Jesus and his struggle to liberate Black people from white oppression. We realize that the Second Covenant may be one of violence, suffering, and sacrifice, because Black people may be called upon to fight their oppressors in a final struggle for survival."*

I had joined a movement for liberation that was embodied in the theology of the Black church.

Nothing made me happier than joining the Shrines of the Black Madonna, but it didn't set well with my father at all.

My father expressed his disapproval many times, often citing misinformation that spread through the community about the shrine and its mission.

One day at the dining room table my father told me, "Daughter, I don't think that you should be a member of that church."

"Why, Daddy?" I asked with youthful sassiness.

"Reverend Cleage doesn't like people your color. He only lets light-skinned people in his church."

"Daddy, I don't think that's true. His righthand man, Oscar Hands, is dark-skinned," I argued.

"Shelley, I think you're making a mistake joining that church."

But I could not be dissuaded. My momma never questioned me about the shrine. Without my daddy's blessings, I still chose to remain a member.

In a short time, I learned that the people of the Bible were Black. So, I stopped my daddy in the living room.

"Daddy, did you know the people of the Bible, the prophets, and kings were all Black?" I asked out of curiosity.

"Yes," he answered.

Then, he paused. He continued, "But, there was nothing I could do about it."

His answer left me speechless as he walked away.

For a few years, my daddy was relentless in his persuasion attempts to pull me out of the church. As I walked into the house one day, he was waiting for me. Seated in a living room chair, he spoke to me in a serious tone full of concern.

"Shelley, I always wanted you to live a better life than I did. We were poor in Alabama. Look at me. I can buy my own clothes, my own shoes, and I have money in my pocket. You won't have any of that, daughter!" He was shaking his head as worry furrowed his brow.

I listened to him, but I had no verbal response. I only nodded my head without offering a rebuttal. I believed that my daddy was sincerely concerned and that he wanted me to be okay.

"Get your education. That is the one thing they can't take away from you," he conveyed with deep concern.

Another day, I was totally surprised when he stopped me in the dining room, looked at me sternly, but with the care that only my daddy could give. He began, "Shelley, I am going to leave you alone about that church. There is one thing that I know about you, daughter. You would not be there if you didn't believe in it."

At that moment, I felt that my daddy accepted my decision and maybe somewhere deep in his heart, but unspoken, he was afraid about his middle daughter's life. I believe that my daddy prayed for my safety and well-being.

The Church—A New Community

I believe it was divine timing, because when I joined Reverend Cleage had already made the decision to dedicate his life to building a Nation with young people. No more public debates or speeches. He declared it a waste of time. His attention was on us, and his intention was to teach and train.

Like so many new and younger members, I was supported by "older members," either by age or by their years of membership in the church. Brother and Sister Sykes invited me to their house to eat dinner. To me, they were a power couple. Not only did they organize a food coop each Saturday, shopping for fruits and vegetables, lining up hundreds of bags, and giving instructions of what produce to put in each bag, but Brother Sykes could sing! A reverberating strong tenor, he elevated the energy in the church service to a clapping-and-dancing pitch.

Brother Sykes also played a major role in marriage ceremonies, exclaiming how the women of the church must be protected. Only a small portion is written below.

"People of the village!" he bellowed from the pulpit. "Hear me now! If you so much as harm the hair of my sister, we will kill you."

This was not a physical threat but more so a recognition that women must be honored. And if a man takes one as his wife, the men of the church are watching and holding him accountable in treating her with respect.

Oscar Hands could sing too, a strong bass. He directed the congregation in singing the Black National Anthem with an unwavering demand that it be done with power. And when we didn't, he stopped the music. Standing tall on the top level of the pulpit, he first silently scanned the congregation with eyes of discontent. Then, he began.

"This song tells of our struggles," he spoke in a reprimanding tone. "It is our national anthem. Now, sing it like you know this. Let's start again."

He motioned to the instrumental section to start playing. We sang it this time with vigor. Oscar Hands also chaired finances and counted offerings after church service. Taking young people under his wing, he not only trained them to sing, but he also taught them the processes of counting and recording monies collected by the church.

Members' homes were opened to us, even though they were scattered across Detroit's east and west sides. I visited Reverend Cleage's residence on Stratford, as well as his family's home located in the Boston District. I also visited the homes of General James and Justine Dismuke, Carolyn Cheeks, Raymond and Ann Cheeks, and others. Diane Stewart, the office manager was also one of the members I met. She quietly and intelligently performed her duties with great efficiency and effectiveness. Also she trained others in office procedures.

I met Reverend Cleage's brothers and sisters, Hugh Cleage, Barbara Cleage-Martin, Gladys Cleage-Evans, and Louis Cleage. They too were involved in the work of the church. Hugh Cleage taught photography, picture development, and printing press operations. Barbara Cleage-Martin was the Cultural Center director and trained many in cultural center management. Gladys Cleage-Evans was a Detroit Public Schools teacher. It was she who recommended that the Direct Instruction System for Teaching Arithmetic and Reading (DISTAR) be used in the first nursery program in Detroit. Dr. Louis Cleage didn't train us, but we did go to him for medical issues.

One day I told Reverend Cleage that I wasn't feeling well. He gently pried open my eyes with his fingers and peered into them.

"You need to go see my brother Louis," he told me.

I went the next day. Upon entering the lobby of Dr. Cleage's office, I noticed that it was small with old gray carpet and a security camera (that didn't work) lodged in a ceiling corner. I sat patiently in an armless leather chair awaiting my turn. I think he was also the receptionist because he had a desk in the lobby. An ashtray filled with cigarette butts was on it. He was smoking! Oh, Lord!

My turn arrived. He directed me into the examination room.

"How may I help you?" he asked.

"Reverend Cleage looked into my eyes and told me to come here for an examination." I informed him.

He looked into my eyes carefully. Then he said, "Tell my brother to keep his fingers out of your eyes."

"Now, that was funny!" I softly giggled to myself.

"Take iron pills," he instructed, "and tell my brother to stop working you all to death."

I was now experiencing the love and support of an extended Black community that was friendly, skilled, educated, talented, and willing to share their lives with us.

In those early days, I always wondered why a man accompanied Reverend Cleage. He was about six feet, very dark skinned, with a "don't mess with me" stare. Dressed modestly in a casual shirt and mildly wrinkled pants, doting a thick head of hair screaming to be trimmed, he stood at attention while Reverend Cleage preached. He also escorted him to

Reverend Cleage's slightly battered dark blue Chevrolet. I soon discovered that his name was Beverly, Reverend Cleage's first bodyguard. He was the seed for the upcoming security force that protected members, community, and the church's institutions.

Hubs of Activity—Shrine One and the Cultural Center and Bookstore

Shrine One and the Cultural Center were hubs of activity. Worship service, choir rehearsals, Black theology classes, children's Bible classes, after-school programs, basketball practices, fellowships, and meetings took place in the church. Orientations, new member intake, poets' readings, historians' presentations, artists' exhibits, leadership meetings, sewing classes, yoga, and dance classes kept a steady stream of people traffic through the Cultural Center.

Upon entering the glass doors, each customer was warmly greeted by Cultural Center personnel. One was immediately emersed in thousands of well-organized book displays by numerous African American authors. Glass counters and cases housed colorful, intricately made earrings, bangles, and necklaces. Human-size African sculptures along with face-size masks from Ghana, Senegal, and Nigeria were exhibited. Another section was set aside for African attire, and African designed material that could be purchased by the yard. Frankincense incense floated throughout.

The physical structure of the Cultural Center included three floors. The main floor where all merchandise was on display and could be purchased. The lower level had two multipurpose rooms, a kitchen, and a sewing room filled with approximately twenty sewing machines. A lobby and two large meeting rooms were on the third floor.

The following people all presented at the Cultural Center, and I had the opportunity to hear them.

- Maulana Karenga, the creator of Kwanzaa.
- Asa Hilliard, professor of educational psychology and historian of indigenous ancient African history, specifically Egyptian.
- Nikki Giovanni, well-known African American poet and writer of nonfiction essays on topics of race and social issues.
- Sonia Sanchez, African American poet, writer, and professor and a leading figure in the Black Arts Movement.

- Milton Henry, founder of the Republic of New Afrika advocating for an independent Black-majority country and reparations.
- Stokely Carmichael, prominent organizer in the civil rights movement.
- Dr. Yosef Ben-Jochannan, historian of ancient Africa and the origins of major religions.
- John Henrik Clarke, historian, professor, and pioneer in the creation of Pan-African and Africana studies.

Yoga at the Cultural Center in 1971

Before yoga was vogue, classes were held at the Cultural Center. Several of us, Virginia Smith, Vincent Stewart, Wanda Stewart, Brother Sykes, and Sister Sykes, attended the yoga class with about twenty other attendees. The instructor was Shashonna. She was brown skinned, about five feet, nine inches tall, and slim. Dressed in forest green leotards, Shashonna radiated a mystical aura. Not only could she manipulate her body into a spinal twist, invert it into a head stand and shoulder stand, she could lead one into meditation with a voice that seemed to hypnotize.

As we entered the room, the sweet, relaxing scent of frankincense incense filled the air, the Indian music of unfamiliar chants and chimes echoed from wall to wall, the dimmed lighting immediately transported us into a new space, leaving behind the outside world. We laid out our towels serving as yoga mats and began to stretch. After a few minutes, Shashonna then spoke.

"Namaste. Let us stand for the sun salutation. Feet together, hands extended with palms turned upward, inhale and lift your hands up toward the ceiling. Bend back. Exhale as you stretch your bodies downward toward your toes."

Shashonna was very direct in her instruction. She demonstrated the yoga postures. Then, we mimicked them. During each posture, she directed our breathing.

"Inhale. Hold it. Exhale."

I was extremely interested in yoga and practiced it every night at home. My goal was to master the headstand and the shoulder stand. I finally did after countless attempts. In one of Shashonna's classes, I had an experience unlike any in my twenty-one years. She demonstrated and then directed us in various postures; some were the cobra, the bow, the spinal twist, and the forward bend. After the movements, she led us into meditation, giving us the option to lay in a corpse pose or to sit in a lotus position.

I sat in the lotus position. My legs were crossed. Each foot was positioned on the opposite thigh with the soles turned upward. My back was straight, right hand was placed on my right knee, left hand on my left knee, and index fingers touching the thumbs, forming a circle.

Shashonna spoke.

"Inhale, exhale."

"Go to your feet. Tell your feet to relax."

"Go to your ankles. Tell your ankles to relax, relax, relax."

"Go to your legs. Tell your legs to relax, relax, relax."

She guided us to relax each part of our bodies.

Then, she said, "Listen to the sound of my voice."

"Inhale, exhale."

"Inhale, exhale."

"Close your eyes."

"Listen to the sound of your own breathing. If your mind should stray away, very gently call it back, and listen. Listen to the sound of your own breathing."

While I followed her instruction, suddenly I had an experience. A white ball of hot light ascended from the base of my spine through the top of my head. I felt as if I would explode. But I was still sitting there! Time seemed eternal.

"Slowly open your eyes," she said.

I did as she instructed us—to stand and come forward. We moved as if we were in a trance while quietly making our way to get the cup of steaming hot herbal tea that Shashonna had prepared. Capturing her attention, I explained what I experienced.

She listened, paused, then said, "I didn't think you would have it this soon." But she never told me what it was.

A few years later, I discovered it was kundalini. The latent energy at the base of my spine was activated and traveled up through each chakra, opening them one by one. Chakras are centers of energy in the astral or spiritual body. Humans have seven chakras. The locations and functions are listed in Table 1 (Kushi, 75).

Table 1. Chakra Locations and Functions

Chakra	What It Governs
Base or First Chakra—Base of Spine	Governs the functions of the bladder and rectum, part of the reproductive function; controls part of the nervous and circulatory functions.
Sacral or Second Chakra—Navel Area	Governs intestinal digestion and absorption in the small and large intestines; part of reproductive function.
Solar Plexus or Third Chakra—Solar Plexus	Governs the activities of the stomach, spleen, pancreas, and kidneys.
Heart or Fourth Chakra—Center of Chest	Governs the heart and circulatory activities; charges electromagnetically the blood and body fluids; controls respiratory and digestive functions.
Throat or Fifth Chakra—Center of Throat	Governs the function of respiration and vocalization; motion of the tongue; volume of saliva; bronchial functions.
Aina or Sixth Chakra—Between Eyebrows	Governs control of consciousness and physical reactions.
Crown or Seventh Chakra—Top of the Head	Governs brain cortex and various kinds of consciousness; unified administration of spiritual, mental, and physical activities.

These energy chakras make physical life possible. Intelligent, invisible forces are at work continuously within each human being. Not only do the chakras govern physical and mental bodily functions, they also are the pathway to a higher consciousness.

We are energy beings composed of the energy forces of the universe. This awareness diminishes our ego and opens the door to who we really are. Although I knew I had the experience, I lacked sufficient knowledge of what it was. When one reaches kundalini, it is described as follows: *"Though still operating on the material plane, the yogi has reached a level of existence beyond time, space, and causation"* (Lidell, Narayani, and Rabinovitch, 71).

Although yoga is linked to India, its origins include the spiritual practices of people who migrated there from the Indus Valley. This region included Egypt and Mesopotamia, the homes of African people. The movements and breathing were practiced to integrate mind, body, and spirit in order to realize our true nature. Many churches reject Eastern thought and practices; however, in examining its history, yoga and meditation were spiritual disciplines of which African people played a major role.

When Shashonna announced her decision to resign from being the yoga instructor, Reverend Cleage asked her, "Whom do you recommend to teach the yoga class?"

She answered, "Shelley should teach it."

So, I became a yoga instructor barely out of my teens, at twenty-one years old.

Reverend Cleage understood the importance of spiritual disciplines and made yoga accessible to members free of charge. Until this day, I often think about how much knowledge and understanding he had. I can't even begin to estimate.

The uniqueness of the Shrine of the Black Madonna is that the goal was the liberation of Black people. Incorporating spiritual disciplines as early as the 1970s was intentional. Every decision was aligned with the purpose of changing Black people's minds and behaviors.

IV

The Church as Change Agent

"BCN SEEKS TO CHANGE SLAVES WHO SUFFER NOT ONLY FROM A SLAVE condition but also from a slave mentality. Everywhere in the world Black people are powerless, enslaved by a hostile society which has declared them inferior, and incapable of full participation as equals. Four hundred years of powerlessness and enslavement is a hostile exploitative society had had profound psychological effects upon Black people. We have been incapacitated for effective struggle against our condition by a basic acceptance of the declaration of Black inferiority imposed upon us be our oppressors. The powerless condition which is systematically forced upon us by our oppressor has created the appearance of real inferiority. Our acceptance of Black inferiority and Black powerlessness has created a slave culture, a sub-culture of the powerless, characterized by identification with our oppressor and a futile dream of escape through integration.

To liberate Black people BCN must first be a psychological change agent. Black people must be changed before their condition can be changed. Slaves cannot be liberated until their slave mentality has been changed. Black people in America cannot be liberated until they have broken all ties with the slave culture which expresses their acceptance of both Black inferiority and Black powerlessness. The slave culture dictates a time ritual, a value system, and a life style; and no slave can be liberated while he remains in the slave culture, has one foot in the slave culture, or still lusts after the irresponsibility of the slave culture" (Cleage).

Table 2 is a focus on the Black Church being the change agent by contrasting slave culture behavior patterns and BCN counterculture behavior.

Table 2. BCN: The Black Church as Change Agent

Slave Culture Behavior Patterns Based on the acceptance of the Declaration of Black Inferiority and the Invincibility of the White Race	BCN Counterculture Behavior Based on the rejection of the myth of the Declaration of Black Inferiority and the Invincibility of the White Race
Escapism Attempts to avoid or distort the reality of the slave condition of all Black people.	*Realism*
1. The use of narcotics to initiate a temporary sense of euphoria.	1. We do not use narcotics to escape or distort the reality of our condition.
2. The excessive use of alcohol that leads to a restriction of one's ability to perform a task.	2. We do not utilize alcohol to the point that it will not allow us to fulfill all Nation commitments at 100 percent capacity. No drinking is permitted before or during a Nation assignment.
3. A theology based on other worldly salvation or mystical divine intervention (slave church, Sunni Islam).	3. Our theology is based on transforming conditions ourselves here on earth.
4. The excessive participation and/or observation of sports, television, radio, movies, and records, perpetual bar and party hopping.	4. Television, radio, movies, records, and other forms of mass communication only serve the purpose as information for the struggle or as a recreational outlet after all Nation commitments have been fulfilled. Sports and parties are only used as a basis for fundraising, strengthening group relations, or recreational outlets and never interfere with fulfilling basic Nation commitments.
5. Continually looking for the big break (hit the number, big contract) or environment that is free from pressures and conflict.	5. We utilize programmatic activity and not luck or chance to change our condition.
6. Involvement in "Black Society" (fraternities, sororities, social clubs) as a basis for status and recognition.	6. Our status and prestige are based on developing power for African people and conscious rejection of White standards.
7. Lifestyle based on constant sexual conquests as basis of ego fulfillment and prestige.	7. Sex does not interfere with any Nation commitments, ability to perform those commitments, or violate Section III of the BCN Code.
8. Meaningless reading (pornography, true confessions, comic books, etc.).	8. All reading encompasses material that relates to better involvement in an understanding of the liberation struggle.

Materialism

Lifestyle that is based on constant purchasing of material goods (cars, clothes, houses, TVs, etc.) to feel meaningful and have status.

1. Immediate gratification of material desires.

2. Conspicuous consumption — owning more natural material goods than needed to survive or beyond the financial capacity of an individual.

3. Being in style as a basis of prestige.

4. Feeling of power and prestige related to amount of material goods owned.

Individual

Placing individualism goals and selfish desires above those of the group.

1. Egotism—responding as if one should always be recognized or be the center of attention.

2. Utilizing other Black people to obtain selfish goals.

3. No feeling of responsibility to help someone with their personal problems.

4. Oversensitive to constructive criticism.

5. Totally dominating group sessions and not allowing others to express opinions.

6. Failing to fulfill commitments on time.

7. Authoritarian attitude.

8. Attempts to acquire personal glory through hangups with titles and position.

Material Standards

1. We work to change the powerless condition of African people without immediate material gratification and the only reward being the liberation of Black people.

2. We purchase goods and services based on our basic needs and not personal prestige or distinction.

3. We reject attempts of our oppressor to make us overconsume through yearly style changes.

4. Prestige is based on the strengths and successiveness of the group.

Communalism

1. We accept the fulfillment of group goals as the basis of status and recognition.

2. We accept each Black person as our brother or sister and treat them with love and respect.

3. We have a sincere "shared suffering" emotion for the problems of all Black people and constantly work to resolve one another's problems and difficulties.

4. We are able to accept constructive criticism and seriously work to improve our functioning.

5. We allow others the opportunity to express their opinions and evaluate each idea that is not our own realistically.

6. We always work conscientiously to fulfill all assignments and commitments on time.

7. We accept the necessity of organization, authority, and a well-defined chain of command, realizing that the basis of strong leadership is humility and a willingness to serve.

8. Group goals are primary and personal desires are secondary.

Irresponsibility

Behavior patterns that tend to be inconsistent and reflecting no desire to be accountable.

1. Doing as little as possible or just enough to get by.

2. Reluctance to make decisions.

3. Reluctance to accept assignments.

4. Gossiping.

5. Persistent lateness or absenteeism.

6. Apathy

7. Disorganization.

8. Disregard for weaknesses that do not affect one personally.

Responsibility

1. All BCN members put out work of the highest quality in every area and maintain high performance standards for themselves and others.

2. Brothers and sisters in leadership positions are not reluctant to make decisions within the framework of the BCN Position and Program.

3. We accept all assignments the Nation feels we are qualified to perform.

4. We do not involve ourselves in the malicious discussion of rumors or gossip.

5. All members report to all meetings and assignments on time unless lateness or absence is excused by group leaders or supervisors. All assignments are thoroughly completed on time.

6. We constantly work to maintain high morale within the Nation and destroy negative attitudes and those who would perpetuate them.

7. We work to become more efficient by becoming more organized.

8. We work to resolve all weaknesses and mistakes no matter who is directly responsible or at fault.

IV – The Church as Change Agent

Nonprogrammatic response to oppression.

1. Black rage.

   a. Inability to deal with the realities of having to work, go to school, etc., with the enemy.

   b. Suicidal attempts to engage in violent confrontation.

2. Nonrealistic nonprogrammatic Black Nationalism.

   a. Cultural nationalism—idealistic emphasis on Black symbols.

   b. Marxism as basis for liberation through integration.

3. Futile effort to build functional unity with groups who do not share the same philosophy or objectives.

   a. Integration

   b. Black capitalism

Programmatic responses to oppression

1. We work tirelessly to drain as much as we can from the White system (money and education) so that we can build counterinstitutions and reject impulsive emotional solutions.

2. We use culture to intensify our level of struggle and commitment to programmatic Nation building.

   a. We reject Marxism as a philosophical basis because it omits the basic reality of racial oppression and leads to a militant form of integration.

   b. We work to build bases wherever African people are for the eventual redemption of the Motherland. This is the only programmatic course for African liberation.

3. We use separatism as a basis for building power for African people.

   a. We reject integration as both impossible and undesirable, and we reject the acceptance of the myth of Black inferiority.

   b. We reject capitalism (Black or White) because it breeds opportunism, encourages individualism, and leads to self-destruction.

Slavery Defined

The definition of "chattel slavery" is the enslavement and ownership of human beings and their offspring as property, able to be bought, sold, and forced to work without wage. Africans were brutally forced into chattel slavery by Europeans for hundreds of years.

Today, a more direct definition of a slave is one who is part of a group whose total existence is controlled by another group. Housing, education, wages, food sources, jobs, medical services, security, production, and manufacturing of goods are ways that Black people totally depend on White institutional structures.

The ingenuity of this system is that Black people through jobs and careers help to maintain power for these institutions that we don't control. We get a paycheck and some benefits. Black men and women serve in the military to protect this country. Black teachers instruct from a curriculum that they didn't devise. Others work in retail and food stores at wages that fail to meet the basic needs of food, shelter, and clothing. Black athletes are paid millions but don't control the National Football League or the National Basketball League. Reverend Cleage labeled these as slave jobs. Consciously or unconsciously, we maintain a system that offers some opportunities but exploits and oppresses us at the same time.

Both a chattel slave and the twenty-first-century slave are controlled systematically, dominated by laws and government that attempt to render them powerless. This is done intentionally to maintain power and economic control.

BCN Group Assignment

I was immediately assigned to an action group upon joining. My first group leader was Karega. His job was to support me in my professed commitment to the liberation struggle. Reverend Cleage organized various groups to meet the needs of the church. Each action group had a specific responsibility, some of which included office managers, Cultural Center managers, youth workers, security personnel, and choir members.

My group was one of the choir groups. So, twenty of us, along with two more choir groups, made up a sixty-voice choir. We attended choir practice and sang at church services. I must admit, I would fluctuate singing soprano to tenor depending on who was standing next to me. The choir became known as the Nationnaires. By that time, I was not in the choir and for good reasons.

I was invited to attend a National Council Meeting, which constituted the leadership structure in the early 1970s. The orientation supervisor reported to the council and the approximately twenty group leaders seated around tables that were arranged in a large square shape. He reported that the group assigned to orientation failed miserably.

"The tablecloth was crooked. The red, black, and green candles were out of order. Spots of wine were on the wine trays," he read from his report on the clipboard.

I listened, slowly raised my hand. I was still a new member. Reverend Cleage acknowledged me. I spoke.

"You can't assume that people know. Providing a detailed checklist to each group leader can help them understand what they need to do."

"Make her a group leader!" Reverend Cleage announced.

I didn't become a group leader at that moment, but the time was quickly approaching. Our participation in the group was the major process for changing behaviors.

Reverend Cleage explained the concept of change.

> *"Change for an individual is a process in which there are a number of interdependent variables. 'Time' is determined by the power to control the individual's total environmental experiences. Also, a factor in changing is our ability to interpret and understand. Efforts to change a slave's time ritual depend upon his willingness to voluntarily accept a new set of environmental experiences. These experiences are diametrically opposed to those 'normal' to his powerless slave culture. The group becomes a new environment. The more completely the group can accomplish total control of the individual's environmental experience, the more quickly change is affected."*

Operationalizing the Group Process

Programmatically, the group process was integrated into the schedule, which changed our time rituals and our commitments. Initially, attendance at Bible class and church service on Sunday; participation in group meetings on Monday; recruitment of new members on weekdays; attendance at orientation on Friday; and participation in Kazi on Saturday. These were the initial processes of participating in a movement. Reverend Cleage expressed this through the Black Christian Nationalist Liberation Triangle, the Power Triangle, and the Divine Triangle. These symbols and concepts were easily grasped and understood by members.

The Liberation Triangle

The Liberation Triangle emphasizes basic participation required as a member. All three sides are KiSwahili terms. The requirements were to Kusanya Watu, which means bringing Black people together. Kodi is to contribute monetarily, voluntary taxation to build a Black Nation, the financial basis of the Nation. Kazi is the communal work program.

Each group leader received a weekly report of their group's Kodi offerings. These were the pledges made when joining. The church asked for $10 to Kodi and $10 to Expansion for employed members. For unemployed, the pledge was $5 to Kodi and $5 to Expansion. We shortened it to say 10-10. The group leader read the report out loud.

"Ernest paid 10-10."

"Gail paid 10-10."

"Elaine paid 5-5."

"Robert paid 2.50-2.50"

This continued until all names were called. If someone could not pay their pledge, the group leader would ask, "Dwight, you didn't pay your full pledge. Why?"

"I am still unemployed and that's all I could pay for now," he answered.

"Well, the group will have to collect more money to make our quota," the group leader responded with assurance.

IV – The Church as Change Agent

Then, group members would search their pockets and purses donating bills and coins collecting enough to make their quota.

Group leaders also received a Kusanya Watu report of how many visitors the group had out that Sunday. The report included the names of group members and their visitors' names.

"Keith, you had two people at church."

"Mary, you had five visitors."

"Ann, you didn't have any one out. What happened?"

As some members offered an explanation and that they would do better next time, a lot of clapping went on for those members who had visitors. Eventually, the name for visitors was changed to "malakeo," a KiSwahili term.

Group leaders automatically knew who attended Kazi by observation because the group leader was present. Group members were extremely proud when Kusanya Watu, Kodi, and Kazi were successful. It showed their commitment to the liberation of Black people.

The Power Triangle expresses the concepts that lead to power. This also was developed by Reverend Cleage.

The Power Triangle

The Power Triangle emphasizes the concepts that lead to freedom. All sides are KiSwahili terms. Uhuru, the base, means freedom from domination. The unity of Black people, Umoja, means oneness or unity. Ujamaa means to collectively work together on a common program.

The Divine Triangle exemplifies the importance of the Holy Spirit as the Source of power needed for internal transformation reflected in outward behaviors.

The Divine Triangle

The Divine Triangle consists of the Holy Spirit as the base. The group process and positive righteousness are complementary sides. The Holy Spirit is God Power accessed by the group as members commit themselves to change. The group process aids individuals in changing behaviors, which is the catalyst for positive righteousness, a practice of behaviors based on love and supportive actions toward others.

The KUA Triangle reflects the union of spirit, mind, and body. This union elevates consciousness and awareness of who we are as human beings. KUA is the science of knowing who we already are. This triangle was developed in the 1980s.

The KUA Triangle

Participation in these triangles supported a person's change process.

How one spends his time determines how he lives his life. Time is everything to life. Reverend Cleage believed that people change if their time is spent in activities and events focused on the goal of liberation. Members were required to spend more of their time in learning, working, and participating in the church, in the movement.

IV – The Church as Change Agent

The Chanza Process

In the *Introduction to the BCN Lifestyle* (1975), Reverend Cleage wrote about a requirement to become a member of the Shrine of the Black Madonna.

To join BCN, an applicant is required to understand and accept three basic facts:

1. *The wretched powerless condition of the Black man is now complicated by the immediate threat of genocide because we are no longer useful to our enemy.*

2. *A slave culture which controls our lives with escapist delusions (the dreams of integration on earth and heaven in the sky after death) is both a product of our powerlessness and the basic mechanism which perpetuates our enslavement and our wretched condition.*

3. *BCN offers the only rational answer to our problems by utilizing the Black Church to unite Black people and building power through the creation of counter-institutions and a counter-culture enabling us to break our dependence upon white people and protecting us from genocide.*

An enemy harms, weakens, or seeks to destroy something else, whether it is by the acts of an individual or a governmental system of laws and policies. The term genocide is the deliberate killing of a large group of people, especially those of a particular group or nation.

Oftentimes, the term genocide is dismissed because of a lack of knowledge. I visited the Holocaust Memorial Center. There is a special section that traces the genocide of people, specifically Black people, to this day. It occurs through civil wars in Africa between the same African people where one faction is supported by the United States with artillery. It can occur through the means of incarceration of millions of Black men who die in prison; through medical apartheid; through the creation of poverty, homelessness, and hunger because of minimum wages; through laws and policies that support lynching; and through legislators who gamble with our lives to stay in power.

The realities of 1975 and 2021 haven't changed much. Reverend Cleage acknowledged Black reality and seriously took it to heart so that the intake process of new members would reflect this.

Young people flocked to Shrine One in the 1970s. On any given Sunday, approximately 50 to 100 women and men joined. It became necessary to develop a formal process for the intake of members in the mid-1970s. Reverend Cleage posed a question to about ten of us in a meeting.

"Do you think that a person who joins will have a problem being transported to the Cultural Center to complete his process of membership?" he asked.

While others answered, "Yes," I said, "No."

"If he or she is serious about being a member, I don't think they will have a problem," I explained.

Reverend Cleage decided that transporting new members to another location would occur. However, it would take discussion, training, preparation, and organization. He delegated responsibilities, which were carried out by members.

The Chanza Process, the intake of new membership, was designed for the individual to experience the seriousness of his lifechanging decision. To become a Black Christian Nationalist required understanding and commitment. The Chanza Process exemplified the beginning of a new life. It involved a preliminary stage, which was followed by a formal process.

Preliminary Stage

- A person walking down the aisle during the invitation hymn.
- New members facing the congregation while being welcomed by the minister.
- The group of new members escorted to the Black Theology Room at Shrine One.
- Information about the Chanza Process was presented.
- New members completed index-size membership cards.
- New members instructed to get their belongings or have a friend get them.
- Initially, they loaded vans and cars to be transported to the Cultural Center and Bookstore. Subsequently, after its acquisition, the Chanza Process took place at the BCN National Training Center.

Formal Process

- After arriving at the Chanza location, new members were led into a spacious room.
- A presentation about the history of the Shrine of the Black Madonna accompanied with slides was given by the Chanza coordinator.
- Formal applications were completed as new members enjoyed refreshments.
- Several interview teams, consisting of a chairperson, security, and a secretary were in separate spaces or rooms. After reviewing the applications, the secretary was instructed to bring in the applicant.

Chairperson: Welcome, I am Fundi Dara, and this is a brief interview to complete your membership. This is Sgt. Amir, and this is Fundi Hana. (We all shake hands.) After reviewing your application, we have a couple of questions.

Security: We will first need proof of identification. A driver's license or state identification will work. Thank you.

Chairperson: Thank you for your honesty in indicating that you do use drugs, specifically, marijuana. In BCN, we consider that unproductive to the work that we must do. It is also illegal. Are you willing to give that up?

I notice that you have some skills in office management. These can definitely be utilized.

Secretary: In our church, there is Kodi, voluntary taxation to build a Black Nation. We ask full-time employees to contribute $10 weekly to Kodi, and $10 to Expansion. We ask part-time or unemployed to contribute $5 to Kodi and $5 to Expansion. I notice that you are a full-time employee. Are you willing to pay $10 and $10? (He is handed a pledge card to complete.)

Would you like to pay your offering today?

Chairperson: Do you have any questions for us? (The applicant has an opportunity to do so.)

Chairperson: This completes your Chanza Process. You are assigned to a Basic Training Group and your group leader is Mwalimu Karifu. Welcome to the Shrine of the Black Madonna, and we are pleased that you are now a member. (The team stands, shakes hands with the applicant, and the secretary leads him back to the main room.)

After all have completed each step of the Chanza Process, they are transported to the Shrine to pick up their cars, to a bus stop, or are transported home.

The intent for Chanza was to provide an extraordinary experience. This was not an ordinary endeavor. Individuals were not joining an ordinary church. They were taking the first step to a new life, dedicating themselves to a movement, to uplifting and empowering Black people. This was a serious commitment and Chanza was structured to reinforce that.

Orientation

Members were required to attend orientation, which was initially held on the second floor at the Cultural Center and Bookstore. The room was set up with three rows of orange chairs on the left and right sides of the room arranged in a semi-oval shape, facing one another, and leaving a wide central aisle. A ritual table was placed in the front of the room. Red, black, and green candles, wine and bread trays were all situated on an African patterned tablecloth.

Orientation began with a call and response led by an orientation leader.

"Pamoja Tutashinda," she said loudly.

"Umoja. Ujamaa. Uhuru," all responded.

Pamoja Tutashinda means "together we shall win." Umoja, Ujamaa, Uhuru, mean "unity, collectively working together on a common program, and freedom." This was followed by the recital of the Black Christian Nationalist Creed and a prayer of invocation. Afterward, the Sacrament of Commitment started.

The candles were lit by the orientation leader as she said, "The red, stands for the blood Black people have shed, are shedding, and will continue to shed for the liberation of Black people. The black stands for Black people. Umoja. Oneness. We are an African people. The green stands for the Motherland Africa. The redemption of the Motherland Africa is the cornerstone of the BCN position."

The Sacrament of Commitment followed the lighting of the candles. This sacrament included partaking of the wine and bread, which symbolized the blood and body of Jesus, the Black Messiah. Oftentimes, a lively skit was performed by a specific group.

The highlight of orientation was the lecture given by Reverend Cleage. General James Dismuke, Bernard Kilpatrick, Woodrow Wilson, and Donald Lester also lectured on the topics of "The Black Church as Change Agent," "Introduction to the Black Christian Nationalist Lifestyle," "The Psychology of Powerlessness," "The Liberation, Divine," and "Power Triangles."

Our minds were being opened as we began to identify our own slave culture behaviors of escapism, materialism, and individualism. During those lectures, we often nodded our heads in agreement or widened our eyes in shock when we learned about the psychological damage we suffered because of the brutality of chattel slavery, self-hatred, escapism, violence against our own people, and paranoia. Even though we heard the lectures, we had not fully internalized them.

After Friday night orientations, a group of us made a beeline to Sugar's Bar, which was located next door to the Cultural Center. We ordered hamburgers, beers, and French fries while we lollygagged and partied. How hypocritical? We'd just listened to a lecture about the slave culture and went to the bar anyway. When Reverend Cleage got word of what we did, he issued a directive. "Bars are off-limits."

"All public bars are off-limits to all BCN members (Probationary and Advanced) at all times because they tend to re-establish the old slave culture time rituals and prevent the adoption of the new BCN Time Ritual. (Exception: BCN members who operate a bar or earn their living as musicians, entertainers, or Disc Jockeys. They may not wear the BCN uniform or insignia while on the job.)"

He believed that how we spent our time either contributed to the liberation struggle or was a continuance of escapist slave culture behaviors.

Reverend Cleage observed our twenty-year-old behaviors and recognized our need to socialize. I believe that he thought about it deeply. Possibly he asked himself, "How can I help them to break ties with the slave culture and fulfill their need to socialize?"

Realizing that he took away our entertainment of barhopping and cabarets, he explained. "If I take activities away, then I must replace them with something else within the church."

Subsequently, he organized Cheza, a KiSwahili term, which means, "a brief pause in the struggle." Reverend Cleage further developed this concept to relate to behavior changes that are relevant and connected to the liberation struggle. He wrote the following guidance.

A Cheza is the highest expression of communal social life and must be so structured and executed.

a. Attendance is limited to Advanced Members in good standing. (No visitors or probationary members are permitted.)

b. The Creed and Cheza Pledge must be repeated at 12:00 a.m. on the high point of "Communal Time."

c. Any member not demonstrating a proper BCN image will not be admitted nor permitted to participate.

Now, young people could party within the confines and sanctity of the church while in the context of the liberation struggle.

Cheza was held at least three times a year and for the most part organized around holidays, such as New Year's Eve. A specific group organized and decorated the fellowship hall. Only experienced disc jockeys were assigned, like Masai and Changa; knowing how to keep the party going was a prerequisite. At least one other person, sometimes two, were assigned to purchase liquor.

On Cheza night, an elaborate assortment of beer, wine, vodka, gin, whiskey, and chasers were included on the liquor table and free to all. Individual groups supplied fried chicken, fruit salads, cheese, crackers, specialty spaghetti dishes, pies, and cakes for their own tables. We visited other groups' tables to nibble on their food.

Reverend Cleage was present at every Cheza. A special table was set up for him. Throughout the evening, any member could sit, enjoy a drink, and talk to him. He very seldom danced but his favorite song was "This Masquerade" sung by George Benson, written by Leon Russell.

The DJ played the music. And we danced. And we danced. And the music played. And we danced. About five minutes before the new year's countdown, we locked hands in a huge circle of at least 100 to 150 people for the BCN Cheza Pledge written by Reverend Cleage. A leader was already assigned to read the words while everyone repeated in unison.

The BCN Cheza Pledge

Cheza is a festival celebrating a renewal of the communal love we have for each other. Cheza is a brief pause in the continuing struggle of Nation building, a pause which serves to fan the flame of a growing working Black Nation.

I believe in the mystical powers of the Divine Triangle.

I believe in the raging desire for freedom born of the Holy Spirit.

I believe in the healing powers of the revolutionary BCN group process.

I believe in the transforming power of positive righteousness expressed through The Liberation Triangle.

I pledge to let the power of the Divine Triangle work its wonders in me.

I pledge to bring a Black counter-culture into being by expressing a wider and deeper love and respect for my brothers and sisters in my everyday life.

I feel the love and power of the group passing through my hands and strengthening both heart and mind for the struggle in which we are joined.

I can sense the communal oneness which binds us together in a sacred brotherhood.

In our unity, I can understand the power of African communalism as the positive fulfillment of a people's life.

I pledge to take the power of the Divine Triangle to African people across the world.

May God and the Black Nation be my witness.

I exist to take Black Christian Nationalism to Black people everywhere.

With Cheza now institutionalized in the practices of the church, there was no need for outside parties and bars. This behavior change along with the purpose of orientation was a continuous intentional process. Orientation lectures presented the realities of Black people, the psychological conditioning that restricts productive thoughts about Nation building, and the Black Christian Nationalist Program. Intellectual understanding recreated a new knowledge base and motivation to change our behaviors. How we grew intellectually and how we spent our time were critical to building for ourselves. This meant that more of our time was redirected to allow for involvement in the struggle.

Saturday Schedule

Participation was also required on Saturdays. No longer would this day just be used to sleep in late, shop all day, read the comics, or just do nothing. This time was now organized to align with Nation building. The process included not only participation in a group but also included recruitment of new members, giving monetarily to the upkeep of the church, and helping to expand Black Christian Nationalism by purchasing buildings that served as institutions we controlled.

Saturdays were scheduled for Kazi, a KiSwahili term, which means communal work to build a Black Nation. It began at 9:00 A.M. in the Fellowship Hall at Shrine One, the Mother Shrine. We were required to be in uniform, Alkebu-lan T-shirts and blue jeans. These T-shirts were white with an image of an ankh in red and the words "Alkebu-lan Academy" circling the image. The ankh is an ancient Egyptian symbol representing life and power. Alkebu-lan is the ancient name of Africa. Academy represents the youth program.

A Kazi coordinator led us in the recital of the Black Christian Nationalist Creed, offered a prayer, and then issued group assignments to sweep, mop, and dust sections of the church's interior while other groups were assigned outside to trim hedges, cut grass, and pick up litter.

After completing initial assignments, we were then required to recruit new members, Kusanya Watu. Groups traveled to several Detroit locations, called spots, with leaflets in hand. Reverend Cleage designed and created leaflets in the early 1970s with perfect penmanship. Using masters to write the messages, the leaflets were then printed on ditto copying machines.

Hundreds of leaflets were also mailed. Individuals were assigned to run off leaflets, fold them, and stuff them into labeled envelopes. In the early days, a group of ministers was carrying out these duties and brought a bottle of wine to the assignment. Well, the unexpected happened! As they laughed, talked, and sipped on wine, someone knocked over the bottle, seriously staining leaflets and envelopes—a purplish mess! To redirect this nonproductive behavior, Reverend Cleage issued a directive that there would be no drinking on assignments or before 8:00 P.M.

After leafleting, we returned to the church at 4:00 P.M. for Pato, a KiSwahili term, which means a communal meal. One group in the church prepared it. Menus included fried chicken, hamburgers, French fries, salad, baked beans, and potato salad. We all sat down at six-foot tables, eating, and enjoying one another's company.

While another group was assigned to wash dishes, clean the kitchen, and mop the floors, the remainder left for home. This concluded Kazi. Our participation was the start of changing slave culture time rituals and behaviors.

"Withdrawal from the slave culture involves a total change in the mentality of a slave. It cannot be accomplished alone but only with the help and support of a group which is concerned. Painful group criticism is a basic part of this process. This is the BCN Group Process without which there can be no liberation of Black people anywhere in the world" (Cleage).

Encounters

Encounters served to address some behaviors.

"You must be brutally honest, to help people to change," Reverend Cleage announced many times.

So, encounters were held on a regular basis. The purpose of these encounters was to increase self-awareness and social sensitivity, and to change behavior through interpersonal confrontation, self-disclosure, and strong emotional expression. However, many of us viewed this process as an opportunity for others to attack rather than to support people in their behavioral change. Because of our limited understanding, many of us young members interpreted encounters as a way to criticize them personally or unconsciously from the mindset of self-righteousness. I was nervous and afraid of encounters.

The encounter meeting room was dimly lit, about twenty-five chairs were arranged in a circle. Reverend Cleage sat at the apex.

He began, "Encounters are done to help change behaviors. So, the floor is open to what you perceive as a problem or issue."

I was completely caught off-guard when my name was mentioned.

"She seems to want to do everything," one member said.

"Yes, she addresses other members about how they should participate more," another commented.

"She should practice saying things differently," actually came from someone I thought was my friend.

Each time someone made a comment, I was embarrassed. I listened with a stoic face but on the inside my emotions boiled like a volcano on the verge of eruption. I was completely unaware about how some members felt. I decided to not defend myself and remained silent.

Reverend Cleage intently listened for what seemed like eternity, he finally asked, "So, you all are criticizing her for being ambitious?"

There were no more comments after that. But it wasn't veneration for me. I felt terrible, a pained energy that wasn't easy to shake.

Being young, Christian revolutionaries, we had adopted common phrases when someone failed to uphold their responsibilities.

"Brother, you need to change."

"Sister, you are individualistic."

"Brother, that's slave culture behavior."

"Oh, you are just a wig out," we declared to those who no longer wanted to function in the church, in the liberation struggle.

We were just young! Still not grasping the depth and scope of commitment, we tried very hard in our limited understanding.

Reverend Cleage often said, "A person's commitment is related to the degree of his understanding." He attempted to increase our understanding constantly. It was a lifelong process.

Intellectual Understanding

Those of us who joined the Shrine of the Black Madonna in the late 1960s and early 1970s called Reverend Cleage, the *Master Teacher,* because our eyes and minds were opened through his teachings. We also called him *Rev,* short for Reverend. He believed in disciplined study and sought to expand the knowledge base of all members. We were required to learn from various authors and researchers.

He emphatically told us, "Everything you learned has been a lie."

"A lie, Rev?" we asked.

"Yes," he replied with authority.

"Everything?' we questioned again.

"Everything!" he answered.

Upon joining, members were given a list of at least twenty books to read. Some titles included the following books.

- *The Black Messiah* by Reverend Cleage.
- *The Choice: The Issue of Black Survival in America* by Samuel F. Yette.
- *African Origins of Christianity* by Yosef Ben-Jochannan.
- *African Religions and Philosophies* by John S. Mbiti.
- *Black Bourgeoisie: The Book That Brought the Shock of Self-Revelation to Middle-Class Blacks in America* by E. Franklin Frazier.
- *Introduction to African Civilizations* by John G. Jackson.
- *Who Needs the Negro?* by Sidney M. Wilhelm.
- *Behavior Modification in Education* by Donald L. MacMillan.
- *Philosophy and Opinions of Marcus Garvey* by Marcus Garvey.
- *100 Years of Lynchings* by Ralph Ginzburg.
- *Black Christian Nationalism* by Reverend Cleage.

This study was ongoing. I read books focused on the group process, spiritual growth, and biblical liberation struggles.

- *The Book of Do-In: Exercise for Physical and Spiritual Development* by Michio Kushi.
- *Meditating with Children: The Art of Concentration and Centering* by Deborah Rozman.
- *Awareness: Exploring, Experimenting, Experiencing* by John O. Stevens.

- *The Sivananda Companion to Yoga* by Lucy Lidell with Narayani and Giris Rabinovitch.
- *Joining Together: Group Theory and Group Skills* by David W. Johnson and Frank P. Johnson
- *Chakra Therapy: For Personal Growth and Healing* by Keith Sherwood.
- *The Essene Odyssey: The Mystery of the True Teacher and the Essene Impact on the Shaping of Human Destiny* by Hugh J. Schonfield.
- *The Passover Plot* by Hugh J. Schonfield.

My mind was being restructured!

I had been a Baptist all my life because my father was one. As a young child, I believed the devil was a little red monster with a three-pronged pitchfork, that God and Jesus were White, that I would burn in hellfire if I liked secular music, if I fornicated, and if I danced. He preached all of that.

But nothing could keep me away from Motown. Stevie Wonder, the Temptations, Martha and the Vandellas, and Smokey Robinson. Their songs were played throughout my eastside neighborhood. I memorized every lyric and learned every dance that was out, Green Onions, Hully Gully, the Twist, the Jerk, the Bop, and the Four Corners. When I joined the Shrine, my theological beliefs changed, but my love for Motown remained the same.

Learning about Jesus was very exciting to me. My speculation now is that the relationship Black people have with Jesus is genetic as well as spiritual. I embraced his history, his life. He was dedicated to empowering his people through inner transformation to end outward Roman oppression. This was validated in books such as *The Wilderness Revolt: A New View of the Life and Death of Jesus Based on Ideas and Notes of the Late Bishop James A. Pike,* by Diane Kennedy Pike along with *The Jesus Party* and *The Pentecost Revolution: The Story of the Jesus Party in Israel, AD 36–66*, both by Hugh J. Schonfield, a British scholar who studied the Dead Sea Scrolls. These scrolls are primarily in the hands of White theologians.

The year that Jesus was born (4 BC), 2,000 African Jews were crucified on the walls of Jerusalem. Crucifixion was created by the Romans as an extremely painful torture device for executing people. Jesus was a threat to the Roman Empire and sadly to the African Jews who accepted Roman oppression. Jesus, the Black Messiah, by all accounts was lynched on a cross.

Jesus told Peter in Matthew 16:18, KJV, *"And I say also unto thee, That thou are Peter, and upon this rock I will build my church; and the gates of hell shall not prevail against it."*

Like Jesus, Peter was also crucified but upside down. Every Christian must ask the questions, "Why? Who crucified Peter?" All Jesus' apostles were killed only because they posed a threat to the power of the Roman Empire.

I love a certain Christmas song titled *Mary, Did You Know?* written by Mark Lowry.

Mary, did you know that your baby boy
Would one day walk on water?
Mary, did you know that your baby boy
Would save our sons and daughters?
Did you know that your baby boy
Has come to make you new?
This child that you delivered, will soon deliver you.

That song ignited a deep aching in my heart because I am a Black mother. There are not many references to the excruciating emotional pain Mary felt. I haven't heard a song that expresses the depth of Mary's sense of helplessness as her son was nailed to a cross. Nor have I read a thesis that speaks of the trauma that lingered with her after Jesus' execution. His death has been romanticized and Mary's experience has been ignored.

From a mother of the present to the mother of Jesus in the past, I humbly ask these questions.

"Mary, did you know your baby boy would be brutally whipped and crucified on the cross?"

"Did you know that your baby boy would be mocked and teased by Roman soldiers?"

"Did you know that your baby boy would feel that God abandoned him?'

"Did you know that in your baby boy's last breath, he would cry out, *'My God, why hast thou forsaken me?'*" Matthew 27:46, KJV.

Black mothers, like Mary, never knew that their babies would be sold during slavery. Today's mothers didn't know that our baby boys would be murdered, lynched by the Ku

Klux Klan, and assassinated by the police. Black mothers did not know that our sons would be incarcerated by the millions.

Jesus never said he was God. This was decided on in the Council of Nicaea, which struggled to define him years after his death to make Christianity, a Black man's religion, palatable to the Romans. He was declared God through the concept of the Holy Trinity, God the Father, God the Son, and God the Holy Spirit. Jesus looked very much like our Black sons today.

Until this day, I cannot completely explain the comprehensive knowledge of Reverend Cleage, but I can say with certainty that he required us to study sources that validated who Jesus was. In his book, *Black Christian Nationalism,* he referenced sources, some of which include the following books.

- *The Origin of Life and Death: African Creation Myths* by Ulli Beier.
- *The Dawn of Conscience* by James Henry Breasted.
- *Development of Religion and Thought in Ancient Egypt* by James Henry Breasted.
- *Ancient Records of Egypt: The Historical Document* by James Henry Breasted.
- *African Origins of the Major "Western Religions"* by Yosef Ben-Jochannan.
- *Are the Jews a Race?* by Karl Kautsky.

As new knowledge was being internalized, Reverend Cleage also undertook other facets of breaking our identification and ties with our oppressors.

African Names

It had to be difficult to address the growing pangs of young people while at the same time developing the program for liberation. Jaramogi must have burned the midnight oil thinking about this program for liberation. Maybe, there were many questions he pondered.

- How to help these young people sever ties with an enemy system that oppresses and exploits?
- How to guide them toward identification with Black people and the Black experience?
- How to help them break the chains of the slave mentality?

I know these must have been some of the questions that kept him up at night in deep thought with pen in hand, writing extensively. This must have been the process for Reverend

Cleage to decide that we must all get African names to identify with our Motherland Africa and our history. Inevitably, he announced that this is exactly what we would do.

In the latter part of 1971, about twenty of us were sitting around six-foot rectangle tables in the Fellowship Hall at Shrine One. We had a few African naming books that we obtained from the Shrine Cultural Center. We excitedly combed through the books, struggling to pronounce the names, to discover their meanings, and to match African names with personalities.

That glorious day in 1971, still twenty-one years old, I received my African name from George Bell. He named me Monifa Dara Omowale, which means *I have my luck, the beautiful one, and daughter returned home.* There was no pomp or circumstance, but overwhelming joy!

George Bell also named Reverend Cleage, Jaramogi Abebe Agyeman. Jaramogi is a title that means *Liberator of the People. Abebe Agyeman,* his African name, means *Defender and Blessed Man.* All members, whether old or new, received African names. Oscar Hands was named Ola Mwanza; Tommy Williams, Changa; Barbara Martin, Nandi; Brother Sykes, Oginga; Ida, the organist, was named Abeni; James Dismuke, Masai; Justine Dismuke, Olubayo; Barbara Rose, Makunda; Carolyn Kilpatrick, Nataki; Diane Stewart, Nilajah; David Scott, Daudi; Raymond Cheeks, Nkosane; Robert, Diop. Each group adopted the same process to name its members.

That informal African naming experience gave rise to many of us young adults to bestow African names on our children legally at their births. It gave rise to formal African naming ceremonial rituals that left us in awe as the drums were beaten, elaborate African attire being worn, and a proclamation that explicated one had given up the slave culture and earned the right to receive an African name. Reverend Cleage led by example. If members received an African name, so must he.

Ministers Fundi and Mwalimu

On that same day that we selected African names, the ministerial titles of Fundi and Mwalimu were designated and bestowed on individuals. *Fundi* means a female minister skilled in one's trade. *Mwalimu* means a male teacher and minister. So, those of us sitting around the table that day were given the titles of Fundi and Mwalimu. I was now, Fundi Monifa.

Reverend Cleage explicitly stated, "A woman can be a minister in the Shrine of the Black Madonna just as well as a man. They both are on equal standing. If a woman brings her skills and talents to the Nation, she qualifies to be a minister."

He followed up with another announcement.

"It is not a requirement for a minister to preach. Ministers can serve in several capacities."

However, he still pushed women to preach. My first-time preaching was with two other women. He announced, "Fundi Ayodele, Fundi Aida, and Fundi Monifa will preach a fifteen-minute sermonette at Sunday's church service."

The week leading up to the service was one of practice and feedback. Reverend Cleage was seated with about four other ministers in one of the meeting rooms. A wooden podium was located in the front. I didn't want to be the first one to speak. But Reverend Cleage called me first.

"Fundi Monifa, you will go first."

I was extremely nervous as I walked to the podium. I started. I finished.

"Monifa, you need to develop the scripture and clarify your three points," Jaramogi advised me.

Fundi Ayodele followed with her practice. And Fundi Aida was last.

I was excited to be selected to preach and wanted to share this with my father. I called him.

"Daddy, I am going to preach a sermonette at the Shrine this Sunday. Can you come?" I asked.

"No," he answered.

"Women are not supposed to be preachers or stand on the pulpit."

My Daddy's belief, as well as many other ministers, demoted women to serve not as leaders but more so as followers. The leadership rank in the church primarily belonged to men.

That Sunday at Shrine One, the church was packed. The balcony was full. We preached in the same order that we practiced. I was first. Fundi Ayodele and Fundi Aida followed. We were twenty-year-old, Black female ministers, preaching from the pulpit.

Reverend Cleage believed that women are just as qualified as men. In the history of the Shrine, he placed women in leadership positions with equal opportunity to be ordained bishops and cardinals.

Standards of Beauty Redefined

During my childhood, most Black women straightened their hair, including my mother. She would go to a nearby hairdresser. I can't recall the age that she began to straighten my hair, but I can vividly remember the experience. She washed it, dried it completely with a towel, combed the tangles out, sat me in a chair, situated herself behind me in her own chair, lit the eye of the gas stove, placed the straightening comb on the flames, parted my hair, put a spat of grease on it, told me to keep still, put the straightening comb close to my scalp, and with a sizzle, crackle, and pop of the grease, she transformed tight curls into stretched-out straight locks. A few ear burns were part of the process.

But my natural hair was so tightly curled that a little humidity turned my freshly straightened hair back to its natural state. My mother even asked her hairdresser about this.

"Ruby, Shelley's hair doesn't stay straightened long. When she goes out to play, her hair looks like I didn't do it at all."

"Ruth, Shelley's hair has a tight curl pattern. Her hair just returns to where it came from," she told my mother laughing softly.

I had no idea why she would straighten my hair as a child, but I was quick to learn that nappy hair, a natural DNA inheritance from generations of Africans was ugly, not beautiful.

Oftentimes, I was unconscious of how much I identified with White standards of beauty. At eighteen years of age, during my first year at Wayne State University, I remember sitting next to a White female student. I suddenly and keenly became aware that I was comparing myself with her. In my mind I said, *White girl,* I thought, *I can be as pretty as you!*

That thought was shocking to me. I went home and washed my hair that same day. No straightening comb! Yes, my tight curls returned. I mastered the technique and discipline of braiding my long and thick hair every night. But, when morning came, I had a full-blown, Black Afro, larger than Angela Davis'. However, the humidity had a devastating effect! It shrunk my big Afro!

Reverend Cleage taught us that Black is beautiful! Thus, he walked forward with his mission to create a transformative culture. So, he strongly suggested that we wear our natural hair. He further explained it as breaking ties with White standards of beauty and loving and embracing our own beautiful selves.

He spoke about the myth of Black inferiority; that we were declared inferior by White oppressors and slaveholders because of the color of our skin, the shape of our noses, and the texture of our hair. But that is only a myth! It was done to justify the evil institution of slavery and the barbaric treatment perpetrated on Black people! When I think about it, I become incensed! Who do they think they are, defining me? Who gave them the right to declare my parents, my grandparents, and my babies inferior? What gave them the idea to defy God who created us this way?

Many of the young people in the Shrine at that time began to marry and have children. Reverend Cleage's teachings guided us to reassure our children that everything about them was beautiful! To institutionalize the breaking of ties with White standards of beauty, he issued guidelines for children residing in Mtoto House, the church's children's institution. These included restrictions of using chemicals, relaxers, or any processes that altered the texture of their hair.

The children wore their natural hair from birth through high school to be in accordance with the directive. I don't think they specifically liked it, especially when they entered high school. However, the new standard of beauty had been set, practiced by their parents, and now passed down to their children. For me, I felt such a powerful identification and an amazing sense of pride with hundreds of Black women wearing their natural hair and sharing the same belief that we could liberate Black people.

Negative Belief System

Jaramogi Abebe Agyeman was insistent and consistent about teaching. He further explained that this negative belief about our hair was a carryover from the slave plantation and from the White man's myth declaring Black people to be inferior. Through a brutal behavior modification process of torturing, lynching, whipping, and murdering Black people into submissive behaviors, our self-image changed. We no longer viewed ourselves through the eyes of a proud African people but through the eyes of the oppressor who declared our natural features as ugly.

Shockingly, we did the same. Jaramogi explained this as a psychological sickness of "self-hatred," which unconsciously motivates us to mistreat other Black people by condemning nappy hair and dark skin. We used descriptions that were demeaning, not uplifting, such as bitches, whores, and dogs. To counter this, Jaramogi tediously developed documents, one of which was the BCN Lifestyle that explicitly clarified how we were to act. The intent was to change our behaviors. The belief was if behaviors could be changed, then beliefs would change also.

"You do what you believe. And you believe what you do!" He mentioned this more than one hundred times.

"Nation building is more than a notion," Reverend Cleage often said. A negative belief system is not only changed through rules and guidelines but through the experiences of God as cosmic energy and creative intelligence and through communal living. This constitutes an inner change expressed by the revelations of the prophets, of Jesus at the River Jordan, and the disciples at Pentecost.

These teachings enlightened us to the universality of our bodies, the expansiveness of our thoughts, and the miraculous strength of our power. To discover the God within, our real selves are transforming. A relationship with God is a means to empower us to struggle against oppression and to build a Black Nation with power for both our survival and our salvation. Spiritual understanding and an openness to God transforms a negative belief system to a positive one.

Uniforms

To further the change process, uniforms were required. When I joined, everyone wore clothes of their own choice. They were very well-dressed. In 1973, it was announced that uniforms would be worn to church service and orientation.

By this time, the BCN National Training Center had been acquired. Many members decided to become full-time in their work for the church. The purchase of uniforms for full-time people required another level of organization. Jaramogi Abebe and a few other ministers visited Detroit's downtown men's shops to select black suits and red shirts. Cardinal Nandi made suggestions for women's uniforms and designated a place where they could be purchased.

The uniforms were red shirts and black suits, black skirts or pants to be worn at church service and orientation. A dress uniform of white suits and red tops was also selected to be worn on special occasions. Alkebu-lan T-shirts and blue jeans were to be worn on Nation assignments.

This trend of purchasing uniforms became a hallmark of the church in all regions. While I was assigned to serve in Houston, Cardinal Olu and I even drove to Dallas, Texas, a four-hour trip, to purchase children's clothes wholesale from a trade market.

The practice of uniformity led to designs of the KUA T-shirt, Black Slate T-shirts, and Summer Camp T-shirts. The purpose of wearing uniforms was to foster traits of unity and loyalty. These are essential for a person as an individual and an organization as a whole to thrive and prosper.

We Are All Leadership

> *"Because we are the leadership vanguard of a world-wide Black liberation movement, we must do everything possible to heighten the distinction between the slave culture lifestyle forced upon Black people by conditions imposed by our enemies, and the BCN Liberation lifestyle which is defined by the nature of our struggle"* (Cleage).

Not too long after I made the statement, "You can't assume that people know," I became a group leader.

I was twenty-one years old. It was by circumstance. Reverend Cleage met with the action group that I was assigned to. About fifteen of us, all in our early twenties, sat in a circle with him, nervously thinking, *Are we about to be dealt with?*

I can't speak for everyone, but I begin to recount in my mind if there was any situation that I had been in that warranted a meeting with Jaramogi. I thought.

"Did I say something? Did anybody in our group do something?"

It was neither one. Jaramogi Abebe began to speak to us.

"Your group leader, Karega, is moving out of town. Who do you think should be your group leader?"

Completely unexpected by me, a few of the members answered, "Monifa. She already acts like she is the group leader."

Honestly, I wasn't trying to become a group leader. I was merely doing what I do. Planning, organizing, holding people accountable, and getting a job done. These attributes were inherited from my parents. They were my blood, my spirit, my inheritance! With that said, I did become a group leader. Never could I have predicted that this was the beginning of a long journey, three decades of my journey to leadership.

Jaramogi told us over and over again, "You are leadership. We all are leadership."

All wasn't easy though. After a couple of years of being a member, I visited Jaramogi because I was troubled. I took the elevator to the seventh floor at the BCN National Training Center, walked down the long hallway, and knocked on his open door. When I entered, I gave him a quick "hell-o." Still standing a few feet in front of him, I poured out my feelings.

"I don't feel productive. I feel like I am mealy mouth—meaning speaking loudly and saying nothing. I cannot put my finger on it, but I am feeling terribly empty."

He remained silent, didn't say a word, and listened to me intently. After I finished ranting, he said, "Monifa, the Nation has stopped developing you."

I was speechless. I left his apartment. But what I reflected on was that he critically examined the effects of the Nation upon my growth. He refrained from being criticizing with expositions about what I should do. He knew me. After that session, each time I turned around, Jaramogi assigned more responsibilities.

Jaramogi tediously assigned and reassigned individuals to areas of responsibility. In my twenties, I was ordained a minister, assigned as a group leader, the administrator of Shrine Two, a member of the National Council, and a member of the Houston Expansion Cadre. Later in my thirties and forties, as with many others, I was ordained a bishop and then a cardinal.

Oftentimes, we would proclaim to one another, "We must be leadership because Jaramogi is getting older."

Yes, we even mentioned this in front of him. Being a man who never hesitated with his words, Jaramogi surprised us one day when he responded, "You all are getting older too."

Levels of Leadership

As the Nation/Church grew, so did the development of the leadership infrastructure. This was an organizational evolution. Shortly after I joined in 1971, Jaramogi was the national chairman who presided over the National Coordinating Committee. To symbolize our unity, the BCN triangular patch was worn on the left upper arm of our black uniform blazers. A second patch that symbolized the growing commitment of members was symbolized by the Total Commitment patch worn on the right side of the black blazer at chest height. My God, did we wear those proudly!

"Look at him. He earned his Total Commitment patch. Look at her. She earned her Total Commitment patch. They are true believers."

Being a church, Jaramogi decided to create ministerial levels of leadership based on a willingness to serve, to act, and to participate in expansion cadres. As the church evolved, these were the governing boards.

Bishops' Council—A group of ordained bishops in each respective region. Their role was to support the membership of that region, to make decisions, and to plan. The Bishops' Council of each region was accountable to the Holy Patriarch.

Assembly of Cardinals—This level eventually replaced the Bishops' Council but served the same role. It consisted of ordained cardinals in each respective region. The Assembly of Cardinals of each region was accountable to the Holy Patriarch.

College of Cardinals—All cardinals belonged to this level. Its purpose was to function as the overall combined leadership of the church. The College of Cardinals was accountable to the Holy Patriarch.

I was ordained a bishop in the 1980s, and a cardinal in the 1990s, which automatically placed me as a member of the regional Assembly of Cardinals in Houston and in the national College of Cardinals.

From 1971 through 1975, the membership of the church increased exponentially in Detroit. It was critical that the foundational tenets of the church as a movement be developed.

Black Christian Nationalism Doctrines

As with all endeavors, especially one as serious as building institutional power, Jaramogi was fully engaged in writing BCN tenets. These texts clarified the mission of the church.

"Being involved in the struggle requires an intellectual understanding not just an emotional response," he often said.

"BCN understands the vicious power reality of the white man's imperialistic, capitalistic, and individualistic society, and fights to free Black men from it by giving a revolutionary programmatic structure and direction to the Black Church by re-affirming the African origins of Christianity and the historic blackness of the biblical Nation Israel and the Black Messiah, Jesus, as the basis of our struggle for African Redemption and the liberation of Black people everywhere" (Cleage).

By 1975, Reverend Cleage had developed the following doctrines. All are summarized here, but the full versions of some are found in the appendices.

I. BCN Statement of Faith—An explanation of the covenant relationship with God beginning with the myth of creation, then identifying the First, Second, and Third Covenants.

II. BCN: The Black Church as Change Agent—An essay that explains the need for Black people to change from a slave condition, and how the Church must serve as a change agent to transform the minds and lives of Black people to make them capable for a liberation struggle.

III. BCN Basic Training Pledge—A statement that outlines a member's acceptance of the myth of inferiority, that Black people are no longer needed by the system, and the requirements for participation in a Basic Training Group.

IV. Criteria for Recycling to a Decision Group—An explanation emphasizing the need to change that is based on objective and subjective evaluation. Failure to meet criteria results in recycling from a Basic Training Group to a Decision Group.

V. BCN Code—A simplified basic statement of the day-to-day behavioral requirements for BCN membership as outlined in the BCN Creed, Program,

Position and Teachings and explained in the books *The Black Messiah* and *Black Christian Nationalism*.

VI. BCN Goals at Basic Training Levels: We Share a Common Past—A tenet that identifies the basic membership levels of the Church: Support Training Group (STG) Level I; Support Training Group (STG) Level II; Basic Training Group (BTG) Level III; Advanced Training Group (ATG) Level IV; and Expansion Cadre (Leadership Level) Level V.

VII. Black Christian Nationalist Glossary—Terminology and meanings.

VIII. Bibliography for BCN Training—A list of required readings.

IX. BCN College Cadre Code—An explanation of the purpose for College Cadres and behavioral requirements.

X. Introduction to the BCN Lifestyle—Requirements for new members and acceptance of three basic facts.

XI. BCN: The Black Church as Change Agent—A contrast of slave culture behavior patterns with BCN counterculture behavior.

XII. BCN Position—Specific statements about the conditions of Black people and involvement in the liberation of Black people.

XIII. BCN Program—An explanation in a series of statements of what BCN seeks and what BCN works for.

XIV. BCN Teaches—An explanation in a series of statements about basic realities and theological position.

XV. BCN Covenant—A declaration of the belief in the Black Messiah, Jesus of Nazareth, and the basis for a collective covenant.

These doctrines were immensely important in reshaping our minds and behaviors. Understanding them created a different mindset, and a frame of reference aligned with the ultimate goal of freedom and power. To attain these, politics played a major role.

V

Politics Are Sacred

"The spirituality of African people encompasses the totality of life. Politics and economics are sacred because they offer programmatic mechanisms for our struggle against white oppression" (Cleage).

LONG BEFORE I BECAME A MEMBER, JARAMOGI WAS HEAVILY INVOLVED in politics. He ran for the governor of Michigan, the first Black man to do so. Oscar Hands, a founder, ran for Wayne County sheriff. Jaramogi taught us that politics were sacred and should be used to better the lives of the Black community. He established the Black Slate, the political arm of the church. Its purpose was to interview potential candidates for office, endorse them, and then support their campaigns. Because he was always in the mode of training, Jaramogi invited us to sit in on the interviews. There, I listened to his questions. I observed his demeanor and learned how to interview political candidates.

In 1974, the Black Slate endorsed Coleman A. Young as the first Black mayoral candidate. Then, the Black Slate Committee organized an immense campaign. Back then, during the early 1970s, Shrine members, including the youth, volunteered to go house to house passing out the Black Slates in all neighborhoods.

On the day of the election, a flurry of excitement was in the air. Over 150 volunteers were assigned to cover major poll locations. We wore black T-shirts with the white, Black Slate emblem across the chest and either black or white pants. Childcare was available.

Food preparers busied themselves in the BCN Training Center kitchen preparing bagged lunches, water, and snacks for poll workers. Church cars and vans were assigned for transportation to the polls. Some were fitted with loudspeakers urging people to go vote! The entire operation was organized in detail.

We were dropped off at poll locations by 7:00 A.M. Designated persons were assigned to bring lunches about noon. We worked the polls until they closed at 7:00 P.M. We were picked up and taken back to the BCN Training Center. Jaramogi was in Room 100 welcoming us back. The flurry of excitement rose even higher as we gathered in the Vanguard Lounge. Fellowshipping, dancing, and having an occasional drink, we waited for the results to be announced. Coleman Young won! That was our victory!

The White police association didn't like Coleman's win as mayor. They threatened to protest by not showing up to work, leaving the city unprotected. Mayor Young contacted Jaramogi. He discussed this dire issue. Immediately, Jaramogi took action. Announcing in church service the details of this situation, he called for 100 volunteers to be trained as police reserves. Instantly, 100 of us stood up. We received instructions to attend training on the use of firearms. We were also scheduled for gun practice at the River Rouge Park gun range. Yes, I participated. I passed the written examination, even received my uniform, peacoat, badge, and master shooter certificate. Jaramogi's belief about politics was paramount to building power.

I participated in candidate interviews in Michigan and Texas. Jaramogi believed in diversity, as long as the candidate proposed to support Black communities. Candidates for governor, mayor, city council, and the schoolboard were interviewed for endorsement by the Black Slate.

It was the political arm of the church and was instrumental in the elections of Mayor Maynard Jackson and Mayor Shirley Franklin in Atlanta, and Mayor Harold Washington in Chicago. Jaramogi was keenly aware of the potential and talent of individuals. He recommended and steered certain members to run for political offices on the schoolboard, the city council, state representatives, and judges. In many cases, these efforts were successful.

"BCN works to create a new independent Black political structure capable of focusing maximum political power in support of the interests of the Black community as defined by BCN" (Cleage).

With development and growth occurring in sectors of the church, the need to build counterinstitutions was also addressed. So, buildings were purchased in order to create and establish a total counterculture.

VI

Building Counterinstitutions

"THE CREATION OF A BLACK COUNTER-CULTURE IN WHICH BLACK counter-institutions make it possible for Black people to survive without total dependence upon white people is an immediate necessity as urgently needed for the survival of white America as it is for the liberation of Black America. Black people must not seek to imitate the kind of materialism which characterizes American life. We do not control the technological-industrial system, the machines, nor the excess capital which makes this possible for our oppressor. Nor do we seek to create for ourselves the quantity of unnecessary goods and services which have become the outstanding characteristic of American life. But unless we can create essential goods and services for ourselves it is futile to attempt to live as though these things are to be provided for us through the generosity of the white man. This will lead only to blind rage and futile confrontation. We must reject materialism, as well as, individualism. We must reject the social disorganization, degradation, and crime of the ghetto and seriously be about the task of changing and rebuilding a people and a community. As Black people we must learn to co-exist in America by building a separate communal existence which enables us to produce the basic necessities of life for ourselves and to build counter-institutions which serve the interests of Black people without threatening the existence of white people. We must return to a simpler way of life which will permit increased independence and self-reliance" (Cleage).

BCN National Training Center

While I was pregnant with my daughter Lateefah in 1972, the church was still moving forward at a fast pace. Jaramogi Abebe Agyeman stated, "If we are to be a nation, we must learn to live together. The church will be purchasing the seven-story Abington Hotel located at 700 Seward in Detroit, Michigan."

This property had an industrial kitchen, a central office, meeting rooms, a bar area (which we later named the Vanguard Lounge), a lower-level huge room (which we named the Hall of Pentecost), a primary meeting space on the first floor, Room 100, a nursery, at least eighty residential units, and an expansive first-floor lobby with cherry wood paneled walls. It was a handsome building.

A wave of excitement rolled across the membership; we are purchasing a hotel! We sacrificed for this; a clear example of how our contributions to expansion were working. We did this! The invitation was extended to all to move in. Young couples were making decisions to leave their houses and rental residences to move into our building, The BCN (Black Christian Nationalist) Training Center and Residence Hall. There was a transition period for the church to assume management responsibilities and for the current residents to move within thirty days.

Security was immediately assigned to protect the building and members who assisted in the transition. Nzapa prepared meals for them on a daily basis. I was about five months pregnant when Jaramogi asked me if I could organize a team to operate the switchboard around the clock.

"Yes," I answered, "I will ask members of my group."

It suddenly struck me that everyone I asked was pregnant. I organized a schedule so each of us would not be so overburdened. Yet in the process, I did not apply that consideration to myself. I took the late-night shifts and slept in a small unit on the seventh floor, which had only a bedroom and a bathroom. It was furnished with a narrow twin bed. The lights were dim, and the walls were dark, but that space allowed me to rest, freshen up, and to take my shifts without traveling back and forth to my house on Wisconsin.

We did operate the switchboard around the clock but at the expense of three of us having our babies early. I was seven months when my daughter Lateefah was born. She only weighed four pounds and four ounces.

I was discharged from Metropolitan Hospital while my baby remained. Then, there was an outbreak of the infectious London flu, and the hospital was quarantined. I still attempted to visit her. My older sister, Vernice, was with me.

"The hospital is on lockdown. There are no visitors," the security guard announced.

I was too shocked and too hurt to say anything. His announcement rendered me speechless.

"But her baby is in there," my sister quickly spoke up.

With caution and compassion, he allowed us to enter.

Lateefah had to stay in an incubator for only a couple of days, because her lungs were sufficiently developed, but she remained in the hospital until she gained enough weight. I visited every day.

"How much does she weigh?" I asked the nurses each time.

In three weeks, she reached five pounds and I could take her home. Thank God, all of our babies survived.

Jaramogi Abebe had no hesitation in asking or assigning us to areas of responsibilities. More often than not, I learned how to organize and complete tasks; definitely these were positive outcomes. The purpose was communal living, so only a thirty-five dollar monthly maintenance fee was charged for members to reside at the BCN National Training Center and Residence Hall. The goal was not to make an enormous profit but to maintain our property.

Moving into the BCN National Training Center

In 1972, from all over the city of Detroit, the Training Center was abuzz with members hauling boxes and furniture into their new apartments. A constant traffic of people walked in and out of the building, chatting and exchanging tidbits of humor. Living there was exciting and energetic.

Members saw one another daily while at the same time engaged in recruiting new members, fulfilling church assignments, accepting roles as group leaders or directors, and participating in the overall work of the church. We had begun the process of learning how to live together. But we were also learning how to build institutions together.

Institutions in Detroit

Expansion was always one of the church's goals as outlined in the BCN Ten Year Projection. We passionately bought into the vision. Working members were asked to pay ten dollars weekly for expansion and unemployed members paid five dollars. Many members met their pledges consistently! Often, Jaramogi would ask for additional pledges in church service to purchase chairs for newly acquired property.

"We are purchasing a building for Shrine Three. We need one hundred and fifty orange chairs. If you can make a pledge, stand up, and announce what it is. Fundi Nilajah will list your pledge. You can pay today," he announced in a worship service.

The majority of members stood up and responded.

In the heart of the city of Detroit and surrounding areas, eleven properties were purchased to serve as BCN institutions. The list follows.

1. Shrine of the Black Madonna #1—The Mother Shrine, Linwood and Hogarth—Church.
2. Shrine of the Black Madonna #2—The Eastside Satellite Shrine, Mack and Burns—Church.
3. Shrine of the Black Madonna #3—The Northwest Satellite Shrine, Wyoming and Seven Mile—Church
4. Shrine of the Black Madonna #4—Technological Center, Photography and Printing Press, Ryan Road.
5. Shrine of the Black Madonna #5—KUA Meditation and The Youth Center, Broad Street.
6. Shrine of the Black Madonna #7—The Kalamazoo Shrine—Church.
7. Shrine of the Black Madonna #8—The Flint Shrine—Church.
8. Shrine of the Black Madonna Bookstore and Cultural Center—Livernois and Davison.
9. BCN National Training Center and Residence Hall, Seward and Second.
10. Cardinal Olu Educational Center, Seward and Second—Meeting Spaces.
11. Residential House, Seward and Second—Member Residence.

All satellite shrines were multipurpose. Church service, group meetings, and events for the public were held there. Other properties served specific purposes, such as printing, youth center, space for spiritual practices, residence for members, and additional meeting spaces.

I was assigned as the administrator of Shrine Two in 1974 at the age of twenty-four. Our first service was a memorial to Malcolm X. On that day, I was busy making sure the chairs were set up, the refreshments ready, and the bulletin properly prepared. Jaramogi stopped me as I dashed passed him.

"Monifa, you have to learn to delegate responsibility," he said.

He was always teaching. Always mentoring. Hundreds of us maintained these institutions. We saw our money at work and our work working! These institutions were purchased, operated, and maintained by Black people!

This speaks of Jaramogi Abebe's leadership. He chose not to live in a mansion on a hill. He chose not to display himself in the most expensive car or adorn himself with overpriced suits. His mind, heart, and soul were focused on building a Black Nation with the in-depth understanding that it had to be done by people.

"People are our greatest resource," he often said. Jaramogi's books, *The Black Messiah* and *Black Christian Nationalism—New Directions for the Black Church,* were read nationally and globally. Persons from Philadelphia, New York, and Chicago were inspired to move to Detroit to join the movement.

The Philadelphia Cadre

In one leadership meeting, Jaramogi shared the news that a group in Philadelphia read *Black Christian Nationalism* and desired to become a part of the church's movement. He appointed Mwalimu Sadikifu to be their group leader and to determine if they were serious about commitment. In a short period of time, they were willing to relocate to Detroit.

Women, men, and children arrived in baggage-packed station wagons. It was New Year Eve's Cheza. I walked out of Shrine One Fellowship Hall and stepped into December's piercing cold to greet the Philadelphia Cadre; Sekou, Morenike, Asha, Major Sele, Kalomo, Mwamba, Sauda, Fundi Kafi, Baye, Kikelimo, and Macharia. The remainder of the cadre, Kambui, Juma, and Hasina remained in Philadelphia.

We called them the Philly Cadre. As our brothers and sisters, we were joined together for the same mission to liberate Black people. Some members of the Philly Cadre were assigned to Expansion Cadres in Atlanta and Houston. They worked in capacities as security, youth workers, and ministers. A few of them have passed on, but their names deserve to be kept alive forever!

New York and Chicago
As the books, *The Black Messiah* and *Black Christian Nationalism*, gained popularity, individuals in New York and Chicago also decided to relocate to Detroit. Askia, Kilolo, Runyararo, Imani, Aombaye, and Akinyele were some of the people from New York. Several came from Chicago. All served with passion.

All shared their talent and knowledge to benefit the growth of the church. Askia assisted Jaramogi Abebe Agyeman in the editing of *Black Christian Nationalism*. Kilolo was the mastermind in organizing fashion show fundraisers that drew crowds of people. Runyararo, Aombaye, and Akinyele were ministers. They lectured, preached, and administered regions.

Institutions in Atlanta, Georgia
Jaramogi Abebe's vision to build a Black Nation with young people became vividly visible as he turned his face toward the south, deciding to expand outside of the state of Michigan, the Central Region. He had always been consistent in announcing and explaining the church's goals. He possessed the leadership qualities of sharing his vision and then rallying individuals to fulfill the goal. All eyes were on Atlanta, the Southern Region!

He had given it considerable thought. One of the steps was to create the Atlanta College Cadre who would relocate to Atlanta, enroll in colleges and universities. Then while studying, invite potential members to become a Black Christian Nationalist, even though there was no physical structure for the Shrine. I am amazed about the faith of these young people barely out of their teenage years, who left Detroit and carved out an existence in Atlanta. They were the pioneers, the preparers of that which was yet to come, The Shrine of the Black Madonna Number Nine. The original cadre was Nneka, Molikai, Menjiwe, Kashaka, and Djenaba.

Establishing a new region required extensive organization. Somehow, Jaramogi had the knack of looking and listening to individuals while identifying their skills and talents, then calling them to action. He wrote, *"Let my failure be due to a lack of ability, rather than to a lack of commitment."*

An invitation was extended to membership to join the Atlanta Cadre. Approximately forty additional members heeded the call and began to prepare at least one year in advance of relocating to Atlanta. Jaramogi held weekly meetings with them for the purpose of preparing their minds and behaviors to function as a cadre, as a group of positively forged relationships with a shared mission. This group became the first Pan African Liberation Corp. During the same time, plans were in place to acquire institutions in Atlanta.

Jaramogi could look at a building and see its potential. An abandoned theater was purchased to become Shrine of the Black Madonna Number Nine. That building had been forgotten, but he envisioned a beautiful, multifunctional church rising out of its ruin. He assigned the Imjimia Cadre, again headed by Kwesi and Changa to restore it. And that they did!

Leaving families for periods of time, they traveled to Atlanta. Hammered late into the night. More properties were purchased to house the Bookstore and Cultural Center, the nursery and youth programs, and an apartment complex for cadre members. After organizing the College Cadre, the Atlanta Cadre, acquiring properties and restoring them, preparations were underway for the 1975 convention, the grand opening of Shrine Number Nine.

Jaramogi's position at the time was national chairman. He headed the National Coordinating Council consisting of Difie, Nilajah, Nataki, Changa, Masai Goree, Zizwe, General Masai, Karamo, and me. A Third Biennial Convention Committee was selected to organize the activities and events of the convention in Atlanta.

Fundi Nataki Mosheshe—Convention Coordinator
Fundi Nilajah Omowale—Transportation and Housing
Sis. Bayo Modupe—Registration
Fundi Monifa Omowale—Publicity and Mailing
General Masai and Colonel Chui—Security

Brother Changa Kagia, Mwalimu Khufu, Sis. Nefertiti Kariuki—Souvenir Booklet

Sis. Kilolo and Bro. Kamau—Fashion Show

Sis. Rashida—Music

Sister Ladjamaya and Difie—Performing Arts

Mwalimu Kwesi Kariuki—Property Manager

Bro. Korkamani and Sis. Olubayo—Missionary Outreach

Sis. Tene Khufu—Alkebu-lan

Mwalimu Akinyele—Public Relations

Sis. Ayanna Nyerere—Cheza Chairman

Mwalimus Zizwe and Sondai—Convention Program

Fundi Nandi—Art Exhibits

Nataki and I flew to Atlanta a few days earlier to solidify preparations. It was the first plane ride for me, at twenty-four years old. On the opening day of the convention, members began to arrive. About 800 people flew in from Detroit on several flights. They were greeted at the airport by a hospitality committee. It was such a wonderful sight to behold; a sea of us dressed in red and black uniforms. Afterward, members were transported to hotels or the residence hall for the weeklong convention. There must have been at least 2,000 people there.

The opening of the convention started with breakfast. Much to our dismay, the caterer failed miserably. They ran out of cheese grits, bacon, sausage, and eggs. Members were hungry and disappointed. Jaramogi told Nataki to find another caterer.

She and I jumped into the car riding through the streets of Atlanta trying to find another caterer. It was pouring down rain. As I looked over at Nataki from the passenger seat, she was crying. I will always remember that day. It was not only raining in Atlanta, Nataki was raining tears in the car. All I could say was, "We will work this out." But we failed to find a caterer.

However, the food problem was resolved. How? Nation cooks took over that responsibility. Groups were assigned to assist in meal preparation. Group leaders contacted their members to serve meals and to clean up. Yes, the group structure prevailed again with success.

The institutions acquired in Atlanta, Georgia, are listed here.
- Shrine of the Black Madonna Nine Church—Ralph Abernathy Boulevard.
- Shrine of the Black Madonna Bookstore and Cultural Center—Ralph Abernathy Boulevard.
- Shrine of the Black Madonna Nursery and Youth Center—Ralph Abernathy Boulevard.
- Three Apartment Complexes—Residence Halls.
- West End Learning Center (2001).

Because of the leadership of Jaramogi Abebe, combined with the total commitment of members, the impossible became possible, the vision became tangible, and the opening of Shrine Nine became real!

When the convention ended, the Atlanta Cadre, the first Pan African Liberation Corp remained. It was 1975. The region grew in membership. Through the effective leadership efforts of Cardinal Sondai and Cardinal Lindiwe, Shrine Nine excelled in productivity, growth, and organization.

Institutions in Houston, Texas

After opening Shrine Nine, Jaramogi Abebe's face turned toward the southwest. Now plans were underway to open Shrine Ten in Houston, Texas, the Southwest Region. It had been only two years since the expansion to Atlanta, Georgia. The call was issued for members to join the Houston cadre. Without hesitation, about forty responded.

This expansion also included the acquisition of properties. Judson Robinson, a city council member and real estate agent, assisted Jaramogi. I can still see that sunny day when Jaramogi, Judson Robinson, security, and I walked a short distance down Martin Luther King Boulevard while Judson pointed out available properties.

With the property business underway, courageously committed men traveled to Houston to start the renovation. The choir stand would be removed and replaced with a spacious pulpit area. The murals designed and painted by a talented African American artist were in progress. What an amazing idea he had in selecting Chimba Chui as the model for the Black Messiah, and Ayanna Abi as the model for the Black Madonna! These murals stretched the entire length of the church's front wall. Both murals depicted dignified power as they towered over the congregation. The signature red carpet, Jaramogi's favorite color, was being laid. While Houston was undergoing physical structural development, the molding of a cadre was also underway.

Jaramogi was keenly aware of the world shifting to technology. So, he asked several young women to apply at companies in Houston for the purpose of being trained in computer skills. Their employment would also be a source of income for the communal budget. He met consistently with the Houston Cadre to map out areas of responsibility and to encounter behaviors that were detrimental to cadre life.

In 1977, the cadre traveled by U-Hauls, airplanes, and cars with the mission of spreading Black Christian Nationalism in Houston. I was actually transferred to Houston the latter part of 1977, three months after the birth of my son, Italo. Temperatures were in the eighties and nineties in November! Humidity was so thick, I felt I could cut it with a knife. It was surprising to see cowboys on horses trampling on main street mediums. To me, Houston was a big country-city. Even with an infant and a five-year-old, I served as a group leader, the Mtoto House coordinator, a nursery houseparent, and the communal budget director.

Mtoto House

The original Mtoto House, although not officially called that, was actually set up in Houston, Texas, in 1977 at 5702 Martin Luther King Boulevard as a means of providing childcare for cadre members. Four apartment units were used as children's residences. These were organized by age and gender. The nursery group, however, was both boys and girls. I was eventually assigned as the coordinator and the nursery group leader of children two to five years old.

I was extremely disappointed at the conditions of the children's apartments. So, one day I talked with Jaramogi about it.

"The Nation is hypocritical," I began respectfully.

"Why would you say that, Monifa?" he asked with a concerned look on his face.

"Because the children's living spaces are not up to par," I answered. "The furniture is shabby. The rooms are not stimulating for children." Then, I continued. "Jaramogi, you said that the Nation would offer us the best life. I don't see it."

He was the type of leader who listened. The very next day, he directed Cardinal Nandi, his sister, and me to shop for new furniture for the children's apartments. Sofas were purchased. Chairs and children's tables were purchased also. The dining room of each apartment was set up as learning centers with bulletin boards, chalkboards, activity books, tape recorders, crayons, notebooks, and children's books.

The Mtoto House in Houston was also an experiment of house parents living with the children six days a week (McIntosh, 2005).

"The only way to learn how to be a houseparent is to experience living with the children," Jaramogi declared.

So, houseparents' beds and belongings were in a two-bedroom apartment that they shared with their age-specific group and spent the night all week. That was indeed a daunting challenge for me! At thirty-two years of age, I was living with the nursery group of nine children, five boys and four little girls ranging from two to four years of age. My twin bed was in the girls' room!

In my whole life, I never dreamed of having nine children! I was the biological mother of only two. I woke my nursery group up two by two each morning, supervised them as they washed their faces and brushed their teeth, ironed their T-shirts and shorts, cooked and served their breakfast, taught them how to make up their beds with their little bitty hands, cleaned the apartment, washed their clothes, cornrowed their hair, and bathed them two by two as I sang, *Jaramogi Abebe is a very great man from the Motherland. Uhuru for freedom! There must be freedom for us.*

I speculate that houseparents Chioneso, Amina, and Idrissa, must have never thought that they would live with groups of children either. But we did! That experiment of living with the children lasted for about a year. It was exhausting!

Houston Pan African Synod

By the time of the Pan African Synod in 1978, hundreds of Houstonians had joined the Shrine because of aggressive new member recruitment spearheaded by Italo Bugat, the Kusanya Watu coordinator.

Organization for this synod was more tedious than the Atlanta Convention. Members, by the hundreds, were arriving from not only Detroit, but Atlanta as well. I served on the hospitality committee. We reserved a large room at the airport, set up with welcome signs, name tags, and hotel assignments. We directed them to specific locations for transportation to hotels, to the residence hall, or to church members who opened their homes. The committee had a printout of air flights.

"Delta Flight 289 from Atlanta is arriving," I announced.

"Delta Flight 180 from Detroit is now landing."

Members stepped off the planes in red and black uniforms. Surge after surge like the continuous motion of the ocean they came! Arriving by cars and vans, thousands flooded Houston, Texas. What an amazing, highly energetic experience!

The synod included information from the Holy Patriarch, Jaramogi Abebe Agyeman, about the directions and theology of the church. Worship services were held. Ministers, bishops, and cardinals were ordained. Kusanya Watu, the recruitment of new members, took place throughout the city. Downtown Houston abounded with members in red and black handing out leaflets with an invitation to visit the Shrine. Childcare was organized. To add to our celebration, Cheza was held. Members from all three regions—Central, Southern, and Southwest—danced, fellowshipped, and chatted. Together, we had accomplished a great feat. We believed we were on our way to build a Nation.

As the synod ended and members returned to their respective regions, much thought was put into the development of the Southwest Region. However, I was reassigned to the Central Region in 1980. There, I served as an Advanced Training Group leader and director of Mtoto House, the children's institution. It was officially established in 1981 by a directive of Jaramogi stating that all regions would set up a twenty-four-hour care of children.

The purpose was to develop them socially, spiritually, physically, and academically. In addition, it was to provide an environment that was safe, secure, racially affirming, and nurturing. Hopefully by living a dormitory-type life, our children would feel a sense of belonging with other children, be loyal, and eventually become the leadership of the church. This process would not only give them a sense of nationhood but also help them to grow as leadership; thus, sustaining the church for generations (McIntosh, 2005).

Southwest Region—The Enclave

In 1986, while in Detroit, Jaramogi asked me to go to Houston.

"Monifa, I would like for you to go to Houston to be in charge of Mtoto House. You don't have to answer now. Just go home and think about it."

That night, I tossed and turned. I prayed. Believing wholeheartedly that I was doing my part to build a better world for Black people, I made my decision. I would go.

It was a Saturday night when I visited Jaramogi in his apartment. Sometimes he would playfully address me by Monifas, instead of Monifa.

"Monifas, look good tomorrow because you will be ordained a bishop," he said with a smile as I started to leave.

That announcement was completely surprising to me. It took a few minutes to settle in. As I walked down the hallway, it finally struck me.

"I am about to be ordained a bishop," I whispered to myself.

Ordination was a reflection of total commitment. On the Sunday I was ordained a bishop in the worship service by the laying on of hands, Ada and Amina were ordained as Fundi, female ministers. All three of us worked with the children. Fundi Ada was assigned as director of Mtoto House in Detroit. Fundi Amina and I were assigned to Houston, Texas. In the next two weeks, we and our families were headed back to Houston in a couple of passenger vans and a U-Haul truck. The year was 1986. I remained in Houston for the next twenty-one years and served as the director of Mtoto House. The implementation of Mtoto House was a daring endeavor to raise "the cream of the crop," the generational leadership that would sustain the nation.

As director of the Mtoto House in Houston, Texas, I faced a heart-wrenching reality. My son, Italo, then in the eighth grade, was having challenges in school. I received his progress report and noticed that his science grade was an "F." The next day, I dressed in an African-designed business suit to talk to his teacher. She informed me that Italo originally had an "A," but that he failed to turn in a science project that was worth four grades.

Stars flashed in my head, butterflies stirred in my stomach, terrified thoughts traveled through my mind about my son's future. Would he become a statistic? Would he end up in jail? Tears uncontrollably flooded my eyes as I tried desperately to hold them back. I finally struggled to say, "What can I do? I have already started him on writing the essay to the project."

"Continue to do that, and he will be graded but he will not get full credit," his teacher answered.

This situation with my son touched me to my core. I decided to talk to Jaramogi.

"I can no longer be the director of Mtoto House. I am responsible for seventy children, but my own son is not doing well in school. He is my son, and he needs me."

He listened. Then he explained, "Monifa if you resign, it will send a disparaging message about Mtoto House across the nation.

My heart and my mind were in battle. I heard and understood what he said.

I sat down with my son that evening. I explained that an "A" can drop to an "F." I illustrated the number of points and percentages for each grade. Then, I told him to complete his essay. He sat at the dining room table looking through encyclopedias. His head began to nod. He could barely keep his eyes open. This was about 11:30 P.M. I said it was okay for him to go to bed and that I would finish his report. So, I stayed up another two hours. I edited, typed his essay, and made it ready for him to submit to his teacher. My son did graduate from high school. He had the highest SAT score.

On that graduation day, as he walked across the stage, it took every ounce of energy in my body to hold me back from running down the aisle with arms flailing, strutting across the stage with him, peering proudly at the audience, and shouting, "We did this!"

I did not resign from being the director of Mtoto House! Eventually, Jaramogi sat down and talked to me.

"Monifa, you have taken Mtoto House as far as you can. You need to go back to college and earn a teacher certification in elementary education," he advised.

I enrolled at the University of Houston main campus shortly afterward. For approximately fifteen years, I lived and participated in an all-Black community run and operated by Black people. I pondered how I would relate to people on campus, including my professors. Knowing that Black people are oppressed by a White-dominated system, which intellectually and emotionally was upsetting to me, I asked myself," Do I overlook the injustices with a smile, or do I carry a frown and maintain my distance?"

The answer was revealed to me. I am a Black Christian Nationalist. The Blackness is my birthright. No conflict with that! Nationalist? I believe in the freedom of Black people. No problem with that either! However, what sparked my awareness was my identification as a Christian. I decided to treat classmates and professors with respect, smiling sincerely and relating positively. Armed with the knowledge of institutional oppression versus daily interactions with a diversity of individuals, my identification remained intact.

I also wondered how I would manage the pressures of attending college full-time while still fulfilling Nation responsibilities. I was a houseparent of nine boys, a group leader of the youth staff, director of Mtoto House, and on the Bishops' Council. After a month of that first semester, I was overwhelmed. I decided to share this with Jaramogi.

"I am going to school full-time taking twelve hours. I also have all of these Nation responsibilities. I don't think I can do both," I said with concern and a bit of guilt.

He listened but then spoke authoritatively. "If you can't figure it out, you will need to quit school."

What? I thought. *Where is the compassion?*

Didn't he advise me to go back? Quitting school was out of the question! So, I figured it out and did both.

Being reflective was something I did often. I posed a question to myself. "Do I wait until I graduate to train the youth staff?"

I was still their group leader. So, my answer was revealed again. Train them with the same knowledge I gained while taking courses. This approach was beneficial for both, because we learned and grew together, improving the academic program for Mtoto House children.

Houston—The Prototype

Jaramogi spent a great deal of time in Houston. His vision was to create a prototype of an urban enclave. With his foresight and the total commitment of many members, the enclave came into fruition. The church strategically purchased nearly all the property, approximately fourteen, on Martin Luther King Boulevard between Old Spanish Trail and Griggs.

1. Shrine of the Black Madonna Number Ten—Church.
2. Shrine of the Black Madonna Training Center—Additional building connected to the Church.
3. Shrine of the Black Madonna Bookstore and Cultural Center.
4. Residence Hall Apartment Complex, 5702 Martin Luther King Boulevard.
5. Residence Hall Apartment Complex, 5400 Martin Luther King Boulevard.
6. Residence Hall Apartment Complex—Missionary Training Institute, 5500 Martin Luther King Boulevard.
7. Apartment Complex, 5666 Martin Luther King (demolished by the church because of previous drug and violent activity, which posed a threat to our security).
8. KUA Meditation Center—Previously a house but renovated into a large room with red carpet to serve as spaces for yoga, meditation, and meetings.
9. KUA Retreat Center—Previously a two-story house with several rooms but renovated and used for yoga, meditation, and meetings. Eventually, it became a member's residence.
10. Marcus Garvey Park.
11. The Thomas Oginga Odinga Sykes Chapel and Kuumba Kitchen (newly constructed).
12. The Alice Strauther Chapel (newly constructed).
13. The Eleanor Hughes Activity Building (newly constructed).
14. The Karamu Group House—a mini two-story mansion with several rooms where devotionals and spiritual practices took place. About ten groups could meet at one time.

Jaramogi spent several years in Houston focused on its development. As with many others, I participated and witnessed the transformation of the Southwest Region where every institution was within walking distance. On any given day, Martin Luther King Boulevard would be flooded with children dressed in red shorts and white KUA T-shirts, walking and running playfully from the Missionary Training Institute to the Training Center during the summer. Or young adults dressed in red and black as they strolled to orientation, group meetings, or church service. Or adults dressed in all white as they sauntered down the street medium for KUA Devotionals and KUA Workshops, or in blue jeans and Alkebu-lan T-shirts each Saturday as they mowed and raked the lawns, trimmed hedges, and swept the property. It was indeed the Sacred Circle, where the power of God is! Even neighbors commented that they felt a sense of safety, security, unity, and power. We believed we were doing the will of God pragmatically and systematically!

One day after we had eaten dinner in the communal dining hall, Jaramogi and I walked through the parking lot that separated two apartment complexes, the residence halls at 5500 and 5400 Martin Luther King Boulevard. It was hot and sunny. He stopped in midstride, paused, and gazed at the buildings.

"Monifa, this would be an ideal place for single mothers to reside. All of their needs would be met," he said.

"Yeah," I thoughtfully responded. "They would have a total support system, shelter, food, and affordable childcare within a safe and nurturing community."

Jaramogi always envisioned a world in which Black people owned counterinstitutions that served all of their needs.

Intensive Teaching

Jaramogi believed wholeheartedly that our knowledge base must change and be expanded to make us capable of struggling for the liberation of Black people. Therefore, he set up several entities over time. These included ministerial training, Black theology classes, preacher training, and discussion groups. Initially, he facilitated each one until a young person (or persons) was trained to do so.

At the Shrine in Houston, he met weekly with a group of ministers in his apartment. These included Olu, Kimathi, Chui, Mbiyu, Ayanna, Lutalo, and me. The meeting started at 9:00 P.M. and, for that reason, I was pleased that refreshments of chicken wings, crackers, cheese, fruit and vegetable trays, and juice were always provided ready for consumption.

At that time, I was assigned to teach Sunday Black theology class, which I did for five years straight. As some of us sat on the sofa, and others on the red carpet, Jaramogi introduced the topic, facilitated a discussion, identified the scriptures, and provided wording for three points. These were to be used in the development of the sermon, the adult Black theology class, and the children's Bible class. In one of these many meetings, the following topics, scriptures, and points were discussed.

Topic: The Vision of a Promised Land
    Scripture: Exodus 14:10–14, NIV

As Pharaoh approached, the Israelites looked up, and there were the Egyptians, marching after them. They were terrified and cried out to the Lord. They said to Moses, "Was it because there were no graves in Egypt that you brought us to the desert to die? What have you done to us by bringing us out of Egypt? Didn't we say to you in Egypt, 'Leave us alone; let us serve the Egyptians'? It would have been better for us to serve the Egyptians than to die in the desert!" Moses answered the people, "Do not be afraid. Stand firm and you will see the deliverance the Lord will bring you today. The Egyptians you see today you will never see again. The Lord will fight for you; you need only to be still."

First Point: The Bible reveals to us the religious struggle of a people who faced the difficult challenges of maintaining the shared vision of a promised land on earth.

Second Point: A people who lack a shared vision find it difficult if not impossible to sustain the tedious, but necessary tasks involved in Nation building. Consequently, they succumb to the same negative forces designed to keep them oppressed and fragmented.

Third Point: The Pan African Orthodox Christian Church calls all Black people to dedicate their lives to the shared vision of a new promised land on earth. Through a Pan African World Community, grounded in communalism, God's power can come to bear to change our earthly conditions (McIntosh, 2001, 121).

Through lengthy discussions, which lasted until midnight or 1:00 A.M., we were able to acquire common interpretations that were taught in Black theology classes and preached in sermons. We put in extremely long hours. Completing Nation assignments during the day, then meeting late into the night.

In one particular preachers' meeting, I arrived and settled on the floor facing Cardinal Olu. He too was sprawled out in a relaxing position.

"Hey, Olu," I said.

"Hey, what's happening, Monifa?" he replied.

"Nothing."

Suddenly, he began to make conversation, which is what he loved to do. I was just tired from teaching and supervising the children. But, for every statement he made, every point he conveyed, I rebutted with a frown on my face. The more I frowned, the angrier he got, raising his voice each time.

Jaramogi, sat in his chair observing the tumultuous situation. Finally, he said, "Monifas!" I turned and faced him.

"You may be speaking the truth 100 percent, but that frown will prevent you from being effective and eventually make the other person mad," he admonished.

Wow. He just chastised me in front of Cardinal Olu. I stopped arguing with him. Then, I took Jaramogi's criticism to heart. I consciously worked on that frown. I definitely wanted to be effective, and I certainly didn't want to make Olu angry. He was my brother, my friend!

Still, after the meeting, the assigned preacher and I had to develop each point.

The two of us met with Jaramogi again on Saturday evening. By that time, I had completed my lesson. But, to our dismay and surprise, he would modify the points.

"Jaramogi, I completed my lesson, typed it up, and made handouts. Now, I have to go back and make changes?" I complained. "It's Saturday evening!"

Before he could respond, I already knew what I had to do. So, I felt a sense of responsibility to complete it, and a sense of accomplishment that I did. I was worn out.

Many of us worked extremely long hours because of our commitment and willingness to do whatever was necessary, whether it was standing security post, cooking communal meals, or caring for the children. Our works were shaped by our religious belief that the liberation struggle was sacred and that each of us had a major role to play.

Expansion to Beulah Land

I can say, without a single doubt, that Jaramogi lived his truth and his calling. The liberation of Black people from oppression and exploitation was his driving force. He developed concise statements of our purpose. *"We are Black. We are oppressed. We seek to end our oppression. Nothing is more sacred than the liberation of Black people."*

So, his face turned toward owning land by which we could grow and harvest crops to feed our communities. A leader knows that he or she cannot build alone. Jaramogi knew this! I detected no overwhelming show of his ego! People were needed, and people were important to accomplish any mission. We were valued. At least, I felt that I was.

Because I was one of those who served on a leadership level, I was privy about his next endeavor. However, it wasn't only his! It was ours! For years, we pledged and sacrificed to raise enough funds to purchase land. Members who have passed on, like Sue Mays, Brother and Sister Sykes, Oscar Hands, and Tommy Williams, contributed thousands of dollars. Those who are still living did the same. Those who missionary outreached braved freezing temperatures and snow in the north and sweltering heat in the south to stand in front of stores collecting money.

On any given Sunday, pledges were taken, and monies were contributed by the majority of members. Jaramogi's nephew, Ernest Martin, was instrumental in identifying land that was to become Beulah Land, the Promised Land! It was not by sheer luck that we made this grand leap. It was because of Jaramogi's vision and the countless number of members who shared that vision. They committed themselves to the work.

Calhoun Falls, South Carolina, was chosen. Five thousand acres were purchased in 1999. Khalfoni and Olatunji willingly changed their college majors to agriculture in order to acquire the knowledge and skills of harvesting catfish and growing crop. Cattle were raised. Hay was rolled. The Order of Nehemiah, brothers and sisters from Detroit, Atlanta, and Houston spent days, weeks, and months committing to construction. They, including Kamau and my late husband Awznee, traveled from Houston to undertake the challenging task of building housing, offices, and meeting spaces.

Jaramogi's mode of operations was consistent. He issued the call for the Beulah Land Cadre and hand-selected others to relocate. Kazi, Badilifu, Niyonu, Muga, Omodele, Nanyamka, Molikai, and Amina were some of the courageous committed ones who answered the call to maintain the land.

Members traveled in droves from the north, the south, and the southwest to the grand opening of Beulah Land in 1999. We walked the land, marveled at the lakes, hugged the trees, rode in open jeeps, gathered for outside meals, listened to speakers, sang the Black National Anthem, offered prayers of gratitude, greeted our brothers and sisters from all regions, and smiled. We were lifted high in spirit and wondrous possibility! This is our land! Let the Black Nation rise!

Expansion and maintenance of properties require consistent funding. A leader's vision, organization, and ability to rally individuals to act are fundamental to the success of any endeavor.

Fundraising

I *remember* and experienced four major forms of fundraising. The major and most sustainable one was giving monies to Kodi, Expansion, and Beulah Land. These primarily came from offerings given by members. Periodically, Jaramogi would announce in church services that pledges were needed to purchase chairs at the satellite shrines. I stood up in service and pledged $200, because I was still employed. Other members also stood up also and pledged.

Expansion Parties

The second method for raising funds was expansion parties. Before the BCN Training Center was acquired, members lived in their own separate homes. But, every Friday night, one Action Group hosted an expansion party at one of these homes. The group purchased, prepared, and sold dinners of fried chicken, fish, and French fries. About forty or fifty of us would gather there, buy the dinners, eat, and fellowship. This method only lasted a short time after we realized that very little money was made as compared to what was spent

Fashion Shows

Our fashion show was one of the most exciting fundraisers. It was held at the Latin Quarters on Grand Boulevard in Detroit. They were always a complete sell-out with crowds wrapped around the block eager to enter. Jaramogi assigned Kilolo, originally from New York, to organize them. She was phenomenal at it!

Kilolo petitioned men and women to model. She collected designer garments. She created the scenes, such as a bar scene while models displayed the latest fashions, or the

African attire scene where models were dressed in the most beautiful and colorful geles, dashikis, and gowns. But the "Honey Patch," the finale scene, stole the show. Models wearing bathing suits strutted to the lyrics of "Slippin' into Darkness" written and performed by War, while a tall, handsome, dark-skinned male model, muscular and shining with baby oil stood at the center of the stage with his arms folded. At the end, he would kneel down, as one special female model positioned herself on his shoulders. He stood up with this queen securely riding on the strength of a king, and the crowd went crazy, clapping for what seemed like hours. In one fashion show, I was selected to be that queen! It was extremely exciting. And quite a lot of money was raised!

Missionary Outreach

The major fundraiser that propelled the rapid expansion of the church was missionary outreach. This idea was presented by Mwalimu Korkamani. After observing people collecting funds at stores, he suggested that we do the same. I clearly remember Cardinal Nandi and Mwalimu Korkamani discussing how this could be done. We first collected money in Kentucky Fried Chicken containers, but that wasn't such a good idea. The second process was to collect money in closed, secured tin cans. They were sixteen-ounce cans in size, with a slot for donations, and a black and white missionary outreach label.

The next challenge was to acquire locations, which we called spots, to collect funds. Group leaders had the responsibility of doing this. Starting in Detroit, group leaders sent their group members downtown, to Kroger's, Kmart, liquor stores, banks, and even the factories when the shift changed at 11:00 P.M. As a group leader, my group would sleep on my living room floor, get up at 10:00 P.M. and travel to the factory to collect from employees. We targeted the men because we knew that they had just gotten paid.

Missionary outreach locations expanded to the Detroit suburbs, then to neighboring states (Illinois, Indiana, Ohio), then to the east coast (Pennsylvania, New Jersey, Connecticut, and New York). My Advanced Training Group even traveled to the Upper Peninsula and crossed over to Canada, bringing back square coins that the counting machine rejected. To acquire spots required calling store managers in many cities asking for permission to post a missionary there to collect funds.

As missionary outreach evolved and became the most profitable fundraiser, teams of four or five were sent out of town, first for one overnight, then two. The job, collect money from 9:00 A.M. to 9:00 P.M. Christmas time missionary outreach was called the "Days of Jesus." Teams were sent out of town from seven days to as many as twenty-one days, only to return on Christmas Eve.

Group competition was strong. There were those who refused to take a break while missionary outreaching. Some brothers collected more than the total of three people. Groups even "spied" on one another to determine if another group raised more money. If by chance they did, then group leaders organized members to go back out and collect again.

On a Wednesday, Jaramogi approached me. "Monifa, would you be willing to take a team out of town Thursday night? "

"Yes, I am willing to do that," I answered.

"You will be the team leader," he continued.

"Okay!"

Four of us, Lukata, Tendai, Nefertiti, and I, went to Pennsylvania. We rented a small red car. It kind of tickled us that it was so small. So, we made up this jingle.

"Going out of town in a little red car. Going over hills and going afar. When we come back, we'll have cash money. Just stand back and call us honey."

I guess Lukata, the only male on the trip, didn't mind the "honey" part.

Young people who performed missionary outreach accelerated the church's goals to expand to Atlanta and Houston, which also expanded the number of cities and states where money was collected. I was unaware of how many millions of dollars the church acquired. All that I know is that through the work of many dedicated Black Christian Nationalists, whose names must always be remembered, never to be forgotten, were the honorable ones who expanded Black Christian Nationalism and its institutions. I can say one thing without a shadow of a doubt. I saw our money being put to good use by the purchase of institutions.

I didn't particularly love to collect money! The mission was bigger than my feeling. *If this action of collecting money is going to ensure a better world,* I thought, *a place of power, a safety zone for my children, then yes, I will do it.*

One weekend, I was missionary outreaching in a suburb of Ohio. It was an amazingly beautiful day, bright skies, radiant sun, and seventy-eight degrees. Standing outside of a Kroger's store with a smile on my face, I began.

"Good morning. How are you? Would you please make a donation to my church's missionary outreach program?" I asked.

Greeting everyone the same way, people dropped quarters and dollars into my can. Then something marvelous happened! I seemed to blend into the energy of this activity. My asking was effortless! The skies and the birds appeared to be in the same spectacular sphere supporting me! I felt a oneness with everything, and it swept over me like a peaceful, blissful breeze. And those shoppers who walked into this sphere gave monies without me asking. I experienced pure joy!

The willingness of many to missionary outreach made it possible to purchase properties. But this venture also required effective leadership. A leader listens! It was wise that Jaramogi took time to hear the ideas and knowledge of others. This quality projected the church forward in acquiring buildings.

Counterculture Construction

Properties were purchased as counterinstitutions. Equally important was the necessity to create a counterculture. Culture is defined at the customary beliefs, social forms, and material traits of a racial, religious, or social group. It is a way of life. In order to change the beliefs and actions of members, groups were given specific purposes. The construction of this shaped members behaviors to align with Nation building. The goals of basic training were organized by levels and summarized below. A more detailed explanation is found in the Appendix I.

Support Training Group (STG) Level I

Belief that BCN is the Answer to the Black people's problems; attend services and events when possible; participation is not total; willing to contribute sacrificially each week.

Support Training Group (STG) Level II

Belief that BCN is the Answer and offers a sound programmatic approach to Black liberation; unable to give total commitment; willing to commit skills; willing to contribute regularly to finance the Black Nation; will support, work, and publicize for Black political power through the Black Slate; willing to run for political office when asked by BCN; willing to support brothers and sisters in Advanced Training and Cadre Levels; know basics of BCN theology; understand the need for communal living.

Basic Training Group (BTG) Level III

Belief that nothing is more important than the liberation of Black people; BCN offers the only sound programmatic approach; belief that I must change discarding slave culture lifestyle, individualism, and the White man's declaration of Black inferiority; belief that I must make a choice between the BCN world of liberation and the world of slavery; belief that my change only occurs through the BCN group process; willing to voluntarily commit to sixteen weeks of training; understand that my change is measured by behavioral objectives, which determines whether I am capable of change.

Advanced Training Group (ATG)

Belief that the group process is still needed after completion of basic training; understand my change is measured by objective criteria of the Liberation Triangle; feel a growing inner commitment and demands of BCN as the instrument for the liberation of Black people; willing to give total commitment to BCN; willing to accept assignment to an Expansion Cadre; willing to take additional training as necessary.

Expansion Cadre (Leadership Level) Level V

Give total commitment to BCN; accept any sacrifice I may be called upon to make; expect to be held accountable for all of my actions; willing to accept disciplinary action if my actions indicate neglect of duty, individualism, revisionism; understand and accept that disciplinary actions at this level may be harsher because it can endanger BCN and the liberation of Black people.

Beliefs and actions of each level made it possible for members to decide their level of participation. In addition, the levels allowed openness to include any BCN member in the liberation struggle. Its major focus is that people are the greatest resource. With each level of membership functioning at its highest capacity, the goal of liberation was a possibility.

In addition to the goals of Basic Training Levels, Holy Orders were formed with specific divine purposes. Jaramogi seemed to always operate with his eye on the prize. His vision propelled him into the future with thought and fortitude. It was like how seasons change. As winter approached, he looked ahead into spring. Again, I joined at the opportune time because I witnessed his creations of Holy Orders. At that time, I did not understand the full scope, but now I know that the purpose was to assist us in our transformation.

Holy Orders were created with specific purposes. Each, in addition, demanded certain behaviors and protocols adding to the processes of creating a counterculture. All were grounded in BCN theology within the divine core that nothing is more sacred than the liberation of Black people. I deemed the Holy Orders as Jaramogi's revelations. From that one bodyguard named Beverly in 1971, a hallowed security force of many was birthed by 1972.

Holy Order of the Maccabees

The Holy Order of the Maccabees was named after the Maccabees in the Apocrypha of the Bible. This book is absent from the King James Version of the Bible. However, it appears in other versions, including the Revised Standard Version and the New Jerusalem Bible.

The book of the Maccabees tells the story of Greek oppression, the looting of the temple, the destruction of Jerusalem, and the massacre of Jews who refused to follow the ordinances of Antiochus, the Greek king. The suffering of the African Jews is reminiscent of Black people today. During this most tragic time, the heroism of the Maccabees is told in their gallant warfare against the Greeks.

"From them came forth a sinful root, Anti'ochus Epiph'anes, son of Anti'ochus the king; he had been a hostage in Rome. He began to reign in the one hundred and thirty-seventh year of the kingdom of the Greeks" (1 Maccabees 1:10, RSV).

"After subduing Egypt, Anti'ochus returned in the one hundred and forty-third year. He went up against Israel and came to Jerusalem with a strong force. He arrogantly entered the sanctuary and took the golden altar, the lampstand for the light, and all its utensils" (1 Maccabees 1:20–21, RSV).

"Israel mourned deeply in every community, rulers and elders groaned, maidens and young men became faint, the beauty of the women faded" (1 Maccabees 1:25–26, RSV).

"In those days Mattathi'as the son of John, son of Sim'eon, a priest of the sons of Jo'arib, moved from Jerusalem and settled in Mo'de-in. He had five sons, John surnamed Gaddi, Simon called Thassi, Judas called Maccabe'us, Elea'zar called Av'aran, and Jonathan called Apphus. He saw the blasphemies being committed in Judah and Jerusalem, and said, "Alas! Why was I born to see this, the ruin of my people, the ruin of the holy city, and to dwell there when it was given over to the enemy, the sanctuary given over to aliens?" (1 Maccabees 2: 1–7, RSV).

The king's officers commanded Mattathias to kill a pig on the sacred altar and to follow the ordinances of King Antiochus.

"But Mattathi'as answered and said in a loud voice: 'Even if all the nations that live under the rule of the king obey him, and have chosen to do his commandments, departing each one from the religion of their fathers, yet I and my sons and my brothers will live by the covenant of our fathers'" (1 Maccabees 2:19–20, RSV).

Instead of succumbing to Greek orders to defy the sacred altar by slaying a pig on it, Mattathias slayed the king's commissioner and the Jew who was willing to do it.

"Then Mattathi'as cried out in the city with a loud voice, saying: "Let every one who is zealous for the law and supports the covenant come out with me!" (1 Maccabees 2:27, RSV).

Immediately afterward he, his five sons, and other men began their warfare against the Greeks to regain their freedom, to recapture their land. When Mattathias was soon to die, he called his five sons together to pronounce his successor so that resistance to Greek oppression would continue after his death.

"Judas Maccabe'us has been a mighty warrior from his youth; he shall command the army for you and fight the battle against the peoples" (1 Maccabees 2:66, RSV).

"Then Judas his son, who was called Maccabe'us, took command in his place. All his brothers and all who had joined his father helped him; they gladly fought for Israel. He extended the glory of his people. Like a giant he put on his breastplate; he girded on his armor of war and waged battles, protecting the host by his sword. He was like a lion in his deeds, like a lion's cub roaring for prey" (1 Maccabees 3: 1–4, RSV).

Judas organized an army ordaining captains over thousands, and hundreds with a fervor to free Israel from Greek oppression. Waging guerilla warfare, the Maccabees won battle after battle, ultimately gaining liberation.

Knowing this history, Jaramogi, in the early 1970s, named the security force of the Shrines of the Black Madonna, the Holy Order of the Maccabees! What a legacy! What a historical and relevant connection to the liberation struggle of Israel.

Jaramogi appointed Masai Balogun to be the first general. We lovingly called him General Masai. He was soft-spoken but full of wisdom and walked with pride, a stately unhurried pace. Smoking a cigar, sitting back in an armchair, he listened without distraction. Reggae was one of his favorite genres. Olubayo, his wife, a leader in the church, was also Caribbean.

General Masai developed the structure, protocols, and tenets of the Maccabees, creating a powerful group of men and women. He attended regular meetings with Jaramogi to discuss each detail of operation. There were positions of majors, sergeants, corporals, lieutenants, privates, and draftees; ordained men and women committed to the protection of the Black Nation.

In everyday wear, the Maccabees were always dressed in pressed uniforms with polished brogans shined so brightly that they reflected light and images. There were also dress uniforms worn to special events and to their promotion services.

At least a month ahead, the announcement of the Maccabee promotions ceremony was listed in the church bulletin. The program was meticulously orchestrated. History of the original Maccabees was read with pride. Judas Maccabeus's courage was exalted. Four Maccabees in dress uniform marched in precision carrying two flags, the Maccabee flag of a gold lion emblazoned on a black backdrop and the red, black, and green flag. Drummers energetically beat bongos and congas as we clapped, tapped our feet, stood, and swayed with the rhythm.

Maccabees dressed as African warriors danced to the beat, sparking latent mind images of our ancestors' dance in our Motherland Africa. Songs were sung and salutes given. In one promotion service, Major Kalomo jumped from the balcony at Shrine One. Surprisingly shocking and spectacular, that act poignantly portrayed the awesome courage and strength of the Maccabees. As each name was called for a promotion, that Maccabee in proud cadence stepped forward. We exploded in applause!

The conclusion of the promotion ceremony was just as awe-inspiring. They trotted in place while lined up one in back of the other. Major Kokayi shouted, "One, two, three!" Then, they moved! Boots thumped against the floor! Filing out in a straight line, marching in perfect synchronization, rhythmically hitting their chests with white gloved fists, they sang.

"*Are*

We are,

We are,

We are,

We are,

We are,

We are

The Maccabees.

Maccabees live on Mount Zion.

BCN is Mount Zion.

Jaramogi rules Mount Zion.

Maccabees defend Mount Zion."

Then they would start the chorus again! Our children stared with wide eyes as they witnessed the presence of a mighty Black army. We all began to sing with pride! When they reached the rear lobby of the church, they broke rank. Jumping and dancing, they chanted in a call and response.

"Pamoja Tutashinda," bellowed one Maccabee.

"Uhuru Sasa," the others roared back.

Its translation is *Together we shall win. Freedom now!*

The Maccabees served to protect and defend. If any situation occurred, such as a car breaking down or someone breaking into a house of my relative, or needing someone to check in on an elderly parent, who did we call? The Maccabees.

In the early morning hour around 2:00 A.M., they made rounds throughout the residence halls to check if every door was locked. Sometimes, I forgot to lock mine. Either still awake or sleeping lightly, I heard the doorknob being turned. The Maccabee would only open the door slightly.

"Security. Door check," he announced.

Then, he would reach his hand on the inside to turn the latch, locking the door. They stood post at every institution, twenty-four seven. In my thirty years as a member, I only remembered the police being called one time! I felt secure. I felt safe. I felt protected! And so it was. Black people protecting Black people.

The Holy Order of Nzinga

In the early 1980s, the Holy Order of Nzinga, a group of women, was ordained to be Keepers of the Holy Spirit and Caretakers of the Children. This Holy Order was named to honor Queen Nzinga (circa 1581–1663) of Ndongo and Matamba located in present-day northern Angola. Born into the ruling family of Ndongo, Nzinga received military and political training as a child, and demonstrated an aptitude for defusing political crises. As a queen warrior, she fought against the slave trade and European influence in the seventeenth century.

"The Warrior Queens of Africa: Nzinga and Mama Yaa Asentewaa" was printed in *The Patriot* in 2014. The following excerpt appears in the article.

> "*The Portuguese slave traders established a fort and settled at Luanda, deliberately encroaching on Mbundu land. Thousands of Ndongo people were taken as prisoners. The king then sent his sister Nzinga Mbandi to negotiate a peace treaty with the Portuguese Governor Joao Corria de Sousa in 1622 to end the hostilities with the Mbundu people. It was at this peace signing conference that Nzinga made herself known for refusing to accept the Portuguese as more superior to her and her people.*
>
> *In preparation for the conference, the Portuguese had a chair for the governor only. They placed a floor mat expecting Nzinga to sit down in subordination to him during negotiations. The historian, Chancellor Williams in his book titled* The Destruction of Black Civilization: Great Issues of Race from 4500 B.C. To 2000 AD *writes: "She took in the situation at a glance with a contemptuous*

smile, while her attendants moved with a swiftness that seemed to suggest they had anticipated this stupid behavior by the Portuguese.

They quickly rolled out a beautifully designed royal carpet they had brought before Nzinga, after which one of them went on all fours and expertly formed himself into a 'royal throne' upon which the princess sat easily without being a strain on her devoted follower. Although a peace treaty was signed successfully between Princess Nzinga and the governor, the Portuguese did not honour it.

The Portuguese attacked Ndongo in 1623. Nzinga was forced to flee when war broke out. She moved north and took over as ruler of the nearby kingdom of Matamba, capturing Queen Mwongo Matamba and routing her army. Nzinga then made Matamba her capital, joining it to the Kingdom of Ndongo. In 1627, after forming alliances with former rival states, she led her army against the Portuguese, initiating a 30-year war against them."

Jaramogi selected Fundi Bayo to be the first Mother Superior. She had this mystical and magical aura that made most feel heard and loved. He also assigned me as the assistant group leader. To prepare for the ordination, we decided to fast. No meals, just water and juice were allowable. About twenty of us gathered in two office rooms at the BCN National Training Center buzzing with excitement. We took body measurements, stretched out red satin material on the floor, laid patterns, and sewed. The red symbolized the flame of the Holy Spirit. A broach of an African crafted stool was adopted in honor of the human stool made by Queen Nzinga's servant.

We worked so hard without food that we became famished with little energy to spare. We were directed by Jaramogi to eat. To still have a sense of fasting, we decided on chocolate candy bars just for the energy.

The ordination was a sight to behold. Twenty women dressed in red satin chemises and flowing ankle-length skirts, each holding a lighted candle, walking in single file, and chanting "Nzinga, My Lord!" Novice, Initiate, and Covenanter were some of the ranks in the Order of Nzinga. It was also established in Atlanta, Georgia, and Houston, Texas, with Cardinals Lindiwe and Ayanna Abi as Mother Superiors, respectively.

To say the least, it was extremely challenging for a group of women to aspire to be like Queen Nzinga, while at the same time doing the inner work to transform ourselves. We recognized that we had not escaped the psychological trauma of slavery and oppression. Feelings of insecurity along with competitiveness surfaced while we were seeking to bond as sisters. This observation was troubling to me.

I decided to talk with Jaramogi about it.

"Why are we all dressed up in red satin with elaborate ordination ceremonies when we still have problems?" I asked out of concern.

"You have to envision what you can become and create experiences that make you feel like you are already there," Jaramogi explained.

In that instance, I believed only a true leader could speak those words. As Keepers of the Holy Spirit and Caretakers of the Youth, the Order of Nzinga worked to fulfill these responsibilities in the Central, Southern, and Southwestern Regions.

The Holy Order of Kuumba

The Holy Order of Kuumba was an adoption of the principle of creativity in the celebration of Kwanzaa. Kwanzaa was created in 1966 by Dr. Maulana Karenga as a festival for African Americans to celebrate the African tradition of the first harvest and to diminish the commercialism of Christmas. It is celebrated from December 26 to January 1.

The seven principles observed and discussed during Kwanzaa are as follows.

1. Umoja—Unity
2. Kujichagulia—Self-Determination
3. Ujima—Collective Work and Responsibility
4. Ujamaa—Cooperative Economics
5. Nia—Purpose
6. Kuumba—Creativity
7. Imani—Faith

Jaramogi fashioned the Holy Order of Kuumba for the purpose of utilizing individuals' creative energies to produce skits and plays that focused on the history, plight, and struggle of African Americans. This group headed by Mwalimu Daudi, was originally called the

BCN Players. They enhanced church services and orientations with dramatic performances.

One of the most well-remembered productions, the Ebony Ritual, was one of the creations of this group. Daudi, Difie, Ladjamaya, and Tiombe, were all master creators. Through collaboration compiled with working late hours, they wrote, produced, directed, and rehearsed. The Ebony Ritual, through prose, song, dance, and poetry eloquently and poignantly told the story of African Americans' journey from Africa to the United States. This production was Broadway quality. Jaramogi nurtured the talent that individuals brought into the church by providing opportunities, time, and spaces for their creative expression.

Holy Order of Nehemiah

The Nehemiah Cadre was founded on the life of the Prophet Nehemiah in the Old Testament. The children of Israel had once again been ravaged by war with many taken into exile by the Persians. As cup bearer to the Persian King Artaxerxes, his job was to test taste the wine before serving it to the king.

The walls of Jerusalem had been destroyed and the city ravaged. He received word from the remnant of those left in Jerusalem.

> *"And they said unto me [Nehemiah], the remnant that are left of the captivity there in the province are in great affliction and reproach: the wall of Jerusalem also is broken down, and the gates thereof are burned with fire. And it came to pass, when I heard these words, that I sat down and wept, and mourned certain days, and fasted, and prayed before the God of heaven, And said, I beseech thee, O Lord God of heaven, the great and terrible God, that keepeth covenant and mercy for them that love him and observe his commandments: Let thine ear now be attentive, and thine eyes open, that thou mayest hear the prayer of thy servant, which I pray before thee now, day and night, for the children of Israel thy servants, and confess the sins of the children of Israel, which we have sinned against: both I and my father's house have sinned"* (Nehemiah 1:3–6, KJV).

Nehemiah's heart and soul were deeply saddened. He longed for the restoration of Jerusalem. He prayed that God would grant mercy upon him and the people of Israel.

> *"And it came to pass in the month Nisan, in the twentieth year of Artaxerxes, the king, that wine was before him: and I took up the wine, and give it unto the king. Now I had not been beforetime sad in his presence"* (Nehemiah 2:1, KJV).

King Artaxerxes asked Nehemiah why he was so sad.

> *"And said unto the king, Let the king live forever: why should not my countenance be sad, when the city, the place of my fathers' sepulchers, lieth waste, and the gates thereof are consumed with fire? Then the king said unto me, For what doest thou make request? So I prayed to the God of heaven. And I said unto the king, if it please the king, and if thy servant has found favor in thy sight, that thou wouldest send me unto Judah, unto the city of my fathers' sepulchers, that I may build it"* (Nehemiah 2:3–5, KJV).

Nehemiah asked for official papers so that Persian governors would allow him access to Judah. Upon arriving at Jerusalem, he told no one about his intent. He viewed the walls of Jerusalem, which were broken down and the gates destroyed by fire. Afterward, he spoke to the group of Jews there.

> *"Then said I unto them, Ye see the distress that we are in, how Jerusalem lieth waste, and the gates thereof are burned with fire: come, and let us build up the wall of Jerusalem, that we be no more a reproach"* (Nehemiah 2:17, KJV).

Organizing a cadre of men, he laid out the plans of rebuilding the walls and to restore the Black Nation Israel to freedom and power.

> *"So built we the wall; and all the wall was joined together unto the half thereof; for the people had a mind to work"* (Nehemiah 4:6. KJV).

Even in the midst of being threatened by Sanballat, Tobiah, the Arabians, the Ammonites, and the Ashdodites, who planned to wage war against them. Nehemiah took action.

> *"Nevertheless, we made our prayer unto our God, and set a watch against them day and night, because of them. Therefore, set I in the lower places behind the wall, and on the higher places, I even set the people after their families with*

their swords, their spears, and their bows. For the builders, every one had his sword by his side, and so builded. So, we laboured in the work: and half of them held the spears from the rising of the morning till the stars appeared" (Nehemiah 4:9, 13, 18, 21, KJV).

Under Nehemiah's leadership, the walls of Jerusalem were restored. This was significant for Israel to gain its freedom and protect the Israelites against their enemies.

To carry on the legacy of the Prophet Nehemiah, the original Imjimia Cadre and Management Company later become the Nehemiah Cadre. The purpose of this skilled group of carpenters, plumbers, and electricians was to renovate and repair the church's property and institutions.

A closed theater in Atlanta, Georgia, was reborn to become Shrine of the Black Madonna Number Nine. An old bowling alley in Houston, Texas, was renovated to an upscale cultural center and bookstore. It was the original group of brothers, first headed by Kwesi, and joined by Gaidi, Ade Amir, Alemu, Hodari, Kehinde, Seve, Okemwa, Orinda, Karega, Nkene, Ilisi, Karamo, Kwame, Amir, and Kofi, that maintained the properties in Detroit. Then some traveled to Atlanta and Houston to renovate, rebuild, and maintain those properties also. In each region, new talent was identified. They too joined in the tasks. Like the walls of Jerusalem, the institutions served as our fortress, as tangible structures of freedom and liberation.

It was ingenious to galvanize the skills, work, talent, and potential of people. But it was even more progressive to trust them as leaders. A wise leader knows that other leaders exist within any organization or endeavor. So, he identifies them. Then, their skills are assessed and are given space to thrive. Jaramogi was one of those wise leaders!

I recall a ministers' meeting in Houston held in his apartment. As ten of us sat on couches and on the red carpeted floor, we shared some passages from the Bible about the prophets of the Old Testament. I was intensely focused on it.

"Jaramogi, you are a prophet," I suddenly said.

He and Kimathi, leaned forward in their chairs.

"What did you say?" Jaramogi asked.

"You are a prophet," I repeated again.

Both Jaramogi and Kimathi veered at me in astonishment. Then, they became silent. Nonchalantly, I lowered my eyes to continue reading more biblical passages. Silence!

I interpreted this silence in two ways. First, that Jaramogi never referred to himself as a prophet. Like others, I had called him Rev. and master teacher. For me to declare him a prophet took him by total surprise that left him speechless. Second, I thought he may have believed that it was God's revelation to me. Possibly, similar to Jesus' experience when he asked Peter, "Whom do men say that I the Son of man am?" found in Matthew 16:13, KJV.

> "When Jesus came to the region of Caesarea Philippi, he asked his disciples, "Who do people say the Son of Man is? They replied, 'Some say John the Baptist, others say Elijah, and still others, Jeremiah or one of the prophets.' 'But what about you,' he asked. 'Who do you say I am?' Simon Peter answered, 'You are the Messiah, the Son of the living God'" (Matthew 16:13–16, NIV).

The difference is that Jaramogi never asked me, "Whom do you say that I am?" Nor did he question me later. Neither did he ever declare that he was a prophet. However, I felt that what we believed about him was very important. I believed he was a prophet.

The Holy Order of the Essenes

The Holy Order of the Essenes consisted of men and women who dedicated their lives to the church's mission full-time. It is the highest level of commitment, as these individuals were willing to accept any assignment, even if it meant relocation. They depended on the communal budget for their existence. And they trusted Jaramogi's promise that if one gives full-time to the church, then the church will provide security from the cradle to the grave. This includes food, shelter, and clothing. Being aware that vision sharing is the foundation of commitment to a cause, Jaramogi devoted time to explain the Essenes as integral communities within the Black Nation Israel.

The history of the Essenes was actually revealed in the Dead Sea Scrolls and the writings of the Jewish historian, Josephus. Also called the Qumran community, they lived in the Judean Desert near the Wadi Qumran, along the northwest shore of the Dead Sea, roughly between 150 BC and AD 68. Their beliefs were firmly entrenched in the covenant relationship with God originating with Abraham.

> *"The LORD had said to Abram, 'Go from your country, your people and your father's household to the land I will show you. I will make you into a great nation, and I will bless you; I will make your name great, and you will be a blessing. I will bless those who bless you, and whoever curses you I will curse, and all peoples on earth will be blessed through you"* (Genesis 12: 1–3, NIV).

This covenant relationship was the foundation of the Jewish religion. Its importance is expressed in their history as shown in the verses found in Exodus and Jeremiah.

> *"I will take you as my own people, and I will be your God. Then you will know that I am the LORD your God, who brought you out from under the yoke of the Egyptians"* (Exodus 6:7, NIV).

> *"So you will be my people, and I will be your God"* (Jeremiah 30:22, NIV).

Upholding the covenant to live as God's chosen people was extremely challenging to the Israelites. Oftentimes, they were influenced by the lifestyles of nations surrounding them. Other times, they worshipped idols. At times, some were not serious about the covenant relationship as they broke the law—the Ten Commandments. They had difficulty establishing themselves with power and sovereignty because of these behaviors.

A number of Jews decided to set themselves apart with a commitment to live as God's holy people worthy of God's blessings. They believed that their pious lives of keeping the covenant would prepare a way for God's intervention. This was their belief in apocalyptic nationalism. Basically, because of their commitment to the covenant, God would intervene by sending a messiah who would free Israel and usher in the kingdom of God, a humane existence in which good prevailed.

The Essenes practiced communal living. Voluntarily accepting a vow of poverty, they had no personal property or money. They ate together, devoted themselves to charity and benevolence, studied the books of the elders, and forbade the expression of anger.

There were hundreds of Essene communities, each specializing in their own craft, such as carpentry, farming, textiles, and pottery making. A system of trade occurred between communities; thereby, creating an economic system independent of the Roman Empire.

Some sources state that Jesus was associated with the Essenes. After his death, the disciples, now the apostles, adopted the same communal belief of the Essenes as shown in Acts 2: 44–46, NIV.

> *"All the believers were together and had everything in common. 45 They sold property and possessions to give to anyone who had need. 46 Every day they continued to meet together in the temple courts. They broke bread in their homes and ate together with glad and sincere hearts."*

These acts by all intentions were to alleviate dependence on the Roman Empire.

The early Christian church established through the apostles was a liberation struggle. After the death of Jesus, 120 individuals consisting of Jesus' disciples, including men and women, received power as a group at Pentecost. This experience of the Holy Spirit empowered them to carry on the work of Jesus.

James, the brother of Jesus, became the leader of the first Christian church during the Apostolic Age after the Pentecost experience. Often called James the Just, he extolled the need to care for the poor, for the wealthy to acknowledge their corruption and accept responsibility for the welfare of the Jewish state, and commitment to liberation from Roman oppression. Possessing the capacity to unite the Jewish factions, he was its greatest leader. These factions include the Zealots, the Sicarii, the Pharisees, the Sadducees, and the Essenes.

The Zealots were a political movement in first century Second Temple Judaism, which sought to incite the people of Judea Province to rebel against the Roman Empire and expel it from the Holy Land by force of arms, most notably during the First Jewish-Roman War (AD 66–70).

Another faction was the Sicarii, a splinter group of the Jewish Zealots who, in the decades preceding Jerusalem's destruction in AD 70, strongly opposed the Roman occupation of Judea and attempted to expel them and their sympathizers from the area.

The Sicarii carried sicae, or small daggers, concealed in their cloaks. At public gatherings, they pulled out these daggers to attack Romans and Roman sympathizers alike, blending into the crowd after the deed to escape detection.

The Pharisees as recorded by Josephus, was a Jewish sect who maintained a simple lifestyle, were affectionate and harmonious in their dealings with others, respectful to their elders, and quite influential throughout the land of Israel. They adhered to laws of which the Deity approves and are considered the most accurate interpreters of the laws. They were also opposed to Roman occupation.

The Sadducees were religious and political. They differed in some aspects of the religious beliefs of the Pharisees. In contrast, the Sadducees believed there is no fate, that God does not commit evil, man has free will of choice of good or evil, the soul is not immortal, there is no after life, and there are no rewards or penalties after death. Politically, they administered the state domestically, represented the state internationally, participated in the Sanhedrin, collected taxes, equipped and led the army, regulated relations with the Roman Empire, and mediated domestic grievances according to Josephus.

Both the Pharisees and the Sadducees held positions in the Temple. The Temple became more than the center of worship in Judea after its reconstruction in 516 BC. It served as the center of society and power. It makes sense, then, that priests held important positions as official leaders of the Temple.

With factions more united under James the Just, a concerted more powerful revolt was waged against the Roman Empire. The Jews were defeated in AD 70 and the second Temple which had existed for 585 years was destroyed by the Romans.

The purpose of the first Christian church has been diluted throughout the ages, making it a tool for escapism as well as to minimize its potential, power, and revolutionary nature. The greatest injustice perpetrated the falsehood that Christianity was a White European religion and that Jesus was White. Then, it was used as a mechanism to pacify Africans during slavery even up until the present times.

The critical role of the Essenes in the liberation of Israel was to implant a communal lifestyle of interdependent communities that would ensure food, shelter, clothing, and care for the Jewish state.

Reflecting on the critical role of the Essenes in the liberation of Israel, Jaramogi ordained full-time members on the communal budget as the Holy Order of the Essenes. Not only did this honor their commitment but also reconnected their lives to the original Essenes. It solidified the belief that our struggle was a holy one, that our lifestyles had to reflect a people worthy of God's power and intercession, that our actions would build a world of freedom, security, and justice for our children and our children's children!

The members of the Holy Order of the Essenes sacrificed their lives. Whether it was five years or thirty years, their willingness made it possible to fulfill the everyday tasks of caring for the children, maintaining the property, securing the institutions, preparing meals, community outreaching, and missionary outreaching. Like many others, I was an Essene for thirty years.

Creating specialized groups was another major component of building a counterculture. Culture has five basic characteristics; (1) it is learned, (2) it is shared, (3) it is based on symbols, (4) it is integrated, and (5) it is dynamic. Cultures share these basic features. Culture is learned. It is not biological. Much of learning culture is unconscious. We learn culture from families, peers, institutions, and media. Constructing a counterculture involved organization of daily life as well as the holidays.

Ramsa Moja and Ramsa Mbili

Ramsa Moja is a KiSwahili term that means the first festival celebrated at Thanksgiving. Ramsa Mbili means the second festival celebrated at Christmas and New Year.

For many of us in expansion cadres, being away from family during these holidays was depressing. On my second assignment to Houston, it was eighty-six degrees on Christmas Day! I had Detroit clothes on, pants, and a long-sleeved turtleneck. Rays of the sun penetrated my clothing. I was sweating profusely on Christmas Day! I missed my parents, my siblings, the smell of pine from the Christmas tree in my mother's living room, the succulent aroma of turkey baking all night in the electric roaster, the cold, and the snow. I missed all of it! So, I did the next best thing. I went to my apartment, lay in the bed, and quietly cried.

Jaramogi had a knack for detecting our emotional moods. Probably, because he was the one who asked us to relocate. He felt a great deal of responsibility about how we were adjusting. In a Bishops' Council meeting, he spoke.

"More must be done to celebrate these holidays both for the psychological well-being of members and the magic of the holidays themselves. From this day on, there will be more effort in celebrating. We need to discuss that now!"

Christmas trees would be placed in the sanctuary and the chapels decorated with red lights, a black ankh as the topper, and a black tree skirt to symbolize the importance of the red, black, and green. All Mtoto Houses would be decorated in the same manner. Children would choose three things they wanted for Christmas. Then, Kimathi, Olu, and the houseparents would shop. They often darted in and out of stores until the midnight hour trying to find exactly what the children wrote on their Christmas lists.

The Festival of Lights would continually be held on Christmas Eve. Hannukah and Advent would be celebrated as well. Observances of these would be done in worship service and the children's institution. We would also missionary outreach an extended number of days but when missionaries returned, grand feasts of turkey, chicken, fish, dressing, macaroni and cheese, greens, cornbread, cranberry sauce, fried corn, salad, green beans, potato salad, and all types of dessert would be served. We would bring in New Year's with Cheza, an evening of refreshments, dancing, and celebration! Through consistent organization and operations around the holidays, spirits were lifted. A home was built away from home!

VII

Communalism—Reflection of Man's Higher Nature

DURING THE PERIOD THAT WE ACQUIRED THE NATIONAL TRAINING Center and Residence Hall, Jaramogi presented another initiative based on communal living. Communalism is a value system of beliefs that places the needs of the group as priority. The purpose is to serve these needs. Obviously, an individual who is a part of that group or people is also served. It is collective wealth shared to feed, house, educate, provide healthcare, and safety for all. In essence, communalism is more aligned with the divine system of God that provides water, fruits, vegetables, and herbs necessary for human life free of charge.

Communalism is diametrically opposed to individualism. For example, in a capitalistic system, a small percentage of the population acquires billions of dollars in wealth either by sale of services or products. The process is structured to exploit and oppress. Whether it is the sale of services or products, capitalism depends on people buying.

Instead of sharing a larger portion of wealth so that all citizens may have basic needs of food, shelter, clothing, and healthcare, as well as have access to a high quality of life with health, happiness, and prosperity, monies are circulated through a few. Policies and laws support profit-making corporations. Poorer people are taxed more while the wealthy have tax breaks by law. Wages, determined by legislators and big businesses, are kept at a bare minimum. Thus, poverty is created.

Communalism is neither Marxist, socialist, nor communist. It is the highest nature of humankind and an expression of the love and nature of God—the Creator. Reverend

Cleage evolved the understanding of communalism to mean the equitable distribution of work, love, and spiritual energy.

> *"The way we live together defines our relationship with God. It requires love and concern for members. It makes fellowship possible. It seeks to enforce renunciation by clearly defining the boundaries separating The Community from the Slave Culture. It seeks to protect the quality of life in The Community—The Kingdom of God on earth"* (Cleage).

The Communal Budget

Jaramogi explained the concept of the communal budget based on African communalism and the apostles' teachings after the death and resurrection of Jesus, and the anointing of the Holy Spirit at Pentecost. The apostles were still engaged in a liberation struggle against the Romans. Uniting with the Essenes who had already set up communities that were self-sufficient, the apostles attempted to do the same in building the church—the movement. In order to break the Black Nation Israel's dependency on the Roman Empire, it was necessary to create a communal economic system to provide for themselves. Acts 2:41–45, NKJV reads as follows.

> *"Then those who gladly received his [Peter] word were baptized; and that day about three thousand souls were added to them. And they continued steadfastly in the apostles' doctrine and fellowship, in the breaking of bread, and in prayers. Then fear came upon every soul, and many wonders and signs were done through the apostles. Now all who believed were together, and had all things in common, and sold their possessions and goods, and divided them among all, as anyone had need."*

Based on the Acts of the Apostles, Jaramogi issued a call for communal living and the need for full-time people.

> *"In order to build a nation, we need people to work full-time. If you bring your talent, skills, energy, and time to the nation, then the church promises security from the cradle to the grave. There will be no salary but all of your needs will be met; food, shelter, clothing, transportation, and childcare by the communal budget."*

He further explained that we must also separate ourselves from the world system that keeps us in debt and exploits our time and talent for the sustainability of an enemy system. Honestly, if the promise did not provide security from the cradle to the grave, I would have rejected the proposition! However, it was more than that. It was a promise, a covenant, based on the premise that people are valued and in return they deserve security.

Many of us quit our jobs and decided to go on the communal budget. Others continued to work and donated their earnings; they received clothing and travel compensations. At the time, I was working for the city of Detroit in the Labor Relations Department as a stenographer. After several months, the Public Relations Department for the Police Department was created. I was transferred there with my young White boss who became the director.

Being what I thought was revolutionary, I defied most rules. Returning from lunch late, wearing short tops instead of tunics, I failed to realize I was making Detroit history by pioneering the Labor Relations Department of the Police Department. My boss was forced to reprimand my nonprofessional behaviors.

"Shelley, I don't ask much of you," he said. "I simply cannot understand why you are late and not abiding by the dress code."

He didn't know that I was searching for meaning and identity. By defying the rules, I was showing my militancy. Needless to say, he had to follow disciplinary procedures and wrote me up. I was suspended for three days. Who knows? I could have run the Public Relations Department at 1300 Beaubien!

Jaramogi also was on the communal budget. The finance reports indicated that he received $300 weekly for necessities. A leader by example, he lived where we lived in the residence halls. He ate in the communal dining halls. These spaces varied by regions. However, the process was the same. Persons were assigned to coordinate the shopping of food and to devise menus. Supervised by a cook, groups prepared the meals. Tables and chairs were set up in a cafeteria style that seated four to eight people. Members lined up to be served by an assigned group. The dining halls were places of connection and chatter.

The communal budget endeavor was challenging. Jaramogi Abebe assigned communal budget directors. I served in this capacity for at least a year. Communal budget directors received a monetary amount to allocate. The process was for members to submit a requisition. For example, if they needed a pair of shoes, the director reviewed it and based on the date submitted and monies available would fill the requisition by placing the monies in an envelope with the person's name on it. Then, it was given to security on duty and kept in a locked closet or deposit box. The member then could pick it up as he signed papers that he received it and was required to submit the receipt.

Oftentimes, the process was smooth and fair. While at other times, some members felt slighted. Their recourse was to inform Jaramogi about their complaint and he interceded to get their needs met. I believed we tried within our young, limited understanding. But that was quite a lot of power, which I had not internalized at the time. To decide whether someone should get shoes, shirts, and pants was not only radical but also risky, because members put their needs and lives in the hands of another. Even in an imperfect process, many needs were met.

After being on the communal budget a few months, I was conflicted about staying on it. I decided to get a job. Without Jaramogi's knowledge, I took an examination at the county, passed it, and was hired as an administrative assistant. Well, after talking with my new supervisor, who was visiting my office, I changed my mind. I worked for one day and decided to resume my Nation duties.

I believe the communal budget was difficult for young fathers who did not have the money to give to their children for field trips, lunch at school, or to personally purchase their clothing. So, that provider instinct was unfulfilled. In hindsight, if certain compensations were permissible for young fathers, then it may have been possible to satisfy that provider instinct. I believe it was also challenging for full-time parents when their children were ready for college with no funds to support them. Or, that our parents were getting older and needed our aid. Even the reality that we were getting older too, how would we be cared for? These were not factored into the communal budget at that time.

Even with its challenges, many of us remained on the communal budget for at least two to three decades. It was a life free of debt, free of bill paying, free of danger, and free of food and economic insecurities. And, on the other hand, it freed us to commit our time, energy, talents, and skills to Nation building. Full-time communal budget members were paramount to the rapid expansion and maintenance of the church's institutions.

Communal Living

Communal living encompassed the totality of our lives. The communal budget was only one component. Because Jaramogi Abebe was intensely focused on the vision of freedom, he identified and analyzed every detail about communal living. These included the dining halls, transportation, childcare, housing, and clothing.

"Why didn't I think of that?" I would often ask myself.

Basically, he set up a structure in which we took care of one another. In Detroit, Cardinal Olubayo was in charge of the dining hall. She supervised a group of people to organize menus, shop for food, and prepare it. Another group was assigned to serve meals, while another cleaned the kitchen and dining hall afterward. Members residing at the BCN National Training Center had the pleasure of eating dinner Monday through Wednesday and on Sunday.

Transportation

For communal transportation, the church purchased a fleet of about fifteen cars, Ford Taurus to be exact, and four vans in Detroit. A special black vehicle was purchased for Jaramogi's use. He didn't own it though. Again, he chose to be on the communal budget because he believed in it as a way of living, as well as a pathway to liberation. The battered dark blue Chevrolet that he previously owned was gone. Because he was our respected leader, security drove and escorted him wherever he needed to go.

In order to use a car, we were required to complete a request-for-transportation form. This was submitted to the director of transportation. Most of the time, it was security. When approved by him, we were handed the keys and the time specifications. The use of vans was primarily for the transportation of our children. They gave the vans simple names, while often yelling out, "I am riding on the blue van. I want to ride on the red van."

With "Shrines of the Black Madonna" painted on the sides, we were proudly recognized throughout the city of Detroit. Subsequently, all three regions had a fleet of cars and vans.

In any nation, the care of children reflects the character of the adult society. To procreate is God's gift to humankind. Then, new life is a miracle, a joy, a sustainability of human beings. When an adult society is keenly aware of this, ultimate attention and care are given to children. They are highly valued. The counterculture of the church took this responsibility seriously.

Children are Wards of the Nation

Jesus said, *"Suffer little children, and forbid them not, to come unto me; for of such is the kingdom of heaven"* (Matthew 19:14, KJV).

Jaramogi, like Jesus, proclaimed that the church/Nation accepts responsibility for the children. He wrote the following. *"All children and young people in the Nation are considered wards of the Nation and under its protection"* (Cleage).

That statement instilled in many of us that all of our work was to ensure a life of power and security for our children. Out of the hundreds of adults who worked directly or indirectly with the children, that lingering light landed in each of our hearts. We are doing this for our children!

A nursery space was immediately set up for two-and-a-half-year-old to four-year-old children. Tene Khufu was the first nursery director at the BCN Training Center in Detroit in 1972. Nefertiti was the assistant. Childcare freed parents to complete Nation assignments or to work in their career jobs. At the same time, the nursery program began the process of molding our children in group life, creating bonds so tight that they remain connected to this day while in their thirties, forties, and fifties.

A reading program was instituted with our nursery children. This idea came from Jaramogi's sister, Gladys Evans, a dedicated Detroit public school teacher. The nursery staff was trained. Due to the major importance of literacy, Jaramogi spoke to those trained individuals.

"Do not debase this program. Follow it in detail," he warned.

Because of its implementation, Direct Instruction for Teaching Arithmetic and Reading (DISTAR), our children read before kindergarten. My daughter, Lateefah, was one of them. There were no childcare fees for full-time people and a minimum fee for others. The church subsidized the care of children as well as the youth programs.

Several youth groups functioned within the church. Some are listed here.
- YTG—Youth Training Group
- BAM—Black Action Movement
- Jael—Teenage, sixteen- to eighteen-year-old girls named after Jael, a heroic woman who killed Sisera, the leader of King Jabin's Canaanite army.
- Machaka—Teenage, sixteen- to eighteen-year-old boys, KiSwahili term, which means African warriors.
- Student Movement—Boys and girls, twelve to fifteen years old.

Each youth group functioned in the larger church community but with programs specific to them. Through orientation and classes, they learned of African history, current Black reality, liberation theology, and tenets of the church. Their schedule included group meetings, and work (Kazi) to maintain the upkeep of the property.

The collective work and contributions of the founders, full-time members, and non-full-time members accelerated the growth of Black Christian Nationalism. All are pillars of history; a unified people were born in the city of Detroit. Many committed their lives in developing BCN in Detroit, then uprooting their lives to expand the church to Atlanta, Georgia, and Houston, Texas. What an ingenious and radical endeavor! A Nation functioning peacefully within a nation!

How can people sustain a nation? How do people actually change, and how is this change sustained? Jaramogi believed that the experience of God transforms people internally, but it also empowers them for a lifelong commitment.

The Holy Spirit

One particular Sunday during service, he abruptly changed the format.

"Today, we are actually going to worship," he announced. "We will chant, 'Lord, strengthen my faith.'"

We begin to chant.

"Lord, strengthen my faith."

"Lord, strengthen my faith."

As we chanted, Chekesha began to sing with the voice of an angel, "God Is" by Rev. James Cleveland.

"God is

My protection

God is

My all and all.

God is

My today and my tomorrow

God, my God is

My all and all.

With eyes closed, I heard people across the aisle cry, scream, and moan. The Holy Spirit to me seemed to travel from the front of the church down the right set of pews. Then, I heard others shout in the back. I continued to chant.

"Lord, strengthen my faith."

The screams and cries got closer as the Spirit seemed to move from the back to the front with the pews on the left side of the church. Tunu was sitting in the pew behind me, and the Spirit hit her. She screamed. I felt it jump from her to me and I cried! The entire congregation was touched. Through our collective invocation, we were able to usher in the Holy Spirit.

I continued to have spiritual experiences. All were not the same. But this experience reminded me of the first few lines of the BCN Creed.

> *"I believe that human society stands under the judgment of one God revealed to all and known by many names. His creative power is visible in the mysteries of the universe, in the revolutionary Holy Spirit which will not long permit men to endure injustice nor to wear the shackles of bondage."*

VIII

The Experience of God

"The group is capable of divine enlightenment which comes with the actual experience of God. The group is both evangelical and revolutionary. Evangelical—The group seeks to bring others into the fellowship because the community alone offers salvation and survival. Revolutionary—The group seeks to bring the world into conformity with the will of God" (Cleage).

KUA—The Science of Becoming What You Already Are!
JARAMOGI SPENT SEVERAL YEARS IN HOUSTON THROUGHOUT THE 1980s and 1990s. Fortunately, I was there during the same time. This allowed me to spend quite a great deal of time under his guidance. He was accessible. He lived where we lived in the residence halls. Monday through Friday, at 3:00 P.M., we knew that we could knock on the door of his apartment. Oftentimes, he would just set a chair right outside of his door. Sitting on the second level porch and taking in the rays of the hot Houston sun, members, including children, would see him.

"Hi, Jaramogi! How are you doing?" they greeted and waved.

Many times, we would just climb those stairs and fill his ears with our woes and concerns.

The concept of KUA was revealed to him. I speculate that this in-depth understanding of spirituality and God Power was expanding with him over the years. The group process which involved encounters and supporting members in their commitment by holding them accountable for their behaviors was and still is a major process of transformation. However, sustained transformation by the experience of God Power resulted in an inner change. Jaramogi emphasized that the experience of God is not an end in itself. It is a means to an end.

"Don't waste the Holy Spirit," he often said.

The ultimate goal is to utilize God Power to change our earthly conditions. It was not enough to say that I am spiritual. It was not enough to proclaim that I spoke in tongues. It was not enough to say that I reached a meditative state. Nor was it enough to say that I mastered the position of standing on my head in yoga.

The goal of KUA was to discover our real selves, our inner divinity, the power within to liberate ourselves. When all titles and layers are peeled away, when all names are discarded, when the ego is controlled, we are universal beings existing and interacting in a divine energy field, which is God. We breathe the energy in, our organs function without our verbal directives, the blood circulates, the ears hear, the eyes see, because they are intelligent. We appear in birth and disappear in death. Knowing who we really are releases potential and power.

KUA Small Group Devotionals

One evening, in a preachers' meeting, Jaramogi challenged us to create a ritual that would involve people in spiritual transformation.

"People need to be in a sustained process that can help open them to the experience of God. I want you all to think about it. Write it down. Afterward, we can discuss it," he explained.

As always, I took on the challenge. I believe I was the only one! I typed up an outline of a ritual based on bits and pieces of rituals previously done. It included prayers, chants, and pacing out of the Sacred Circle. I took the copy to Jaramogi. As he sat quietly perusing it, I intently gazed at his face in order to detect any sign that I had done a good job. He set my paper down on the coffee table, walked into a back room, reentered with a handwritten draft of the KUA Group Devotionals. He read aloud the following.

"KUA Group Devotionals is a systematic, sustained group process that takes a

group of seekers through seven distinct steps to the climatic experience of God in Kugasana. Each step gradually erodes the walls of separation in which the group becomes more open to each other and to God. It is a spiritual journey.

Step 1: *Invocation—We Acknowledge the Presence of God*

Step 2: *Discourse on the Nature of God and What God Expects Us to Do— Covenant Relationship*

Step 3: *We Have Failed to Satisfy Our Covenant Relationship with God— We Are Sinners*

Step 4: *Confession and Penance*

Step 5: *Awareness—To Sharpen Our Perception, which Sharpens Our Perception of Our Relationship with God and with Each Other*

Step 6: *We Stimulate the Energy within (God Incarnate) through Massages/Movements—Sense of Communalism*

Step 7: *We Open Ourselves to the Experience of God, which Is Meditation"*

After he finished reading, he handed the copy to me.

"Type it up and develop each step. In essence, embed substance for each concept. You can include prayers, chants, absolution processes, confession protocols, awareness exercises, yoga, massages, and meditation techniques. We are going to start first with the children in Mtoto House during the eight-week summer camp. Altars will be installed in each Mtoto House apartment. Each time a child looks at the altar, he or she will become aware of the presence of God. Children's attire for KUA Group Devotionals will be black shorts for the boys and black leotards with skirts for the girls. The houseparent of each group will facilitate the devotional."

He gave me quite a lot to do! I began by developing the purpose and processes of each devotional step, as shown in Table 3.

Table 3. Devotional Steps, Purpose, and Process

Steps	Purpose	Process
Step 1: Invocation— We Acknowledge the Presence of God	Awareness of the presence of God within the Sacred Circle and the need for God's healing power.	–Ringing of Sacred Chimes –Chanting –Kutafuta Meditative Response –Prayer of Invocation
Step 2: Discourse on the Nature of God and What God Expects Us to Do—Covenant Relationship	Knowledge of the nature of God and our faith. God is Cosmic Energy and Creative Intelligence.	–Discourse/presentation that illustrates the nature of God and explains what God expects us to do.
Step 3: We Have Failed to Satisfy Our Covenant Relationship with God—We Are Sinners	Awareness that we have alienated others and because of this, we have failed to keep the covenant.	–Confession Sermonette
Step 4: Confession and Penance	Admission that behaviors have diminished our covenant relationship with God and stand guilty of being a barrier to God's power.	–Prayer of Courage –Personal Confessions –Encounter –Purification Prayer –Chant: "Cleanse Me, Oh Lord!" –Absolution: Washing of Hands –Prayer of Absolution –"Bless Us, Oh Lord. Help Us to Do Thy Will."
Step 5: Awareness — We Sharpen Our Perception, which Sharpens Our Perception of Our Relationship with God and with Each Other.	Grow increasingly aware of sensations, emotions, thoughts, and physical energies.	–Awareness Exercises
Step 6: We Stimulate the Energy within (God Incarnate) through Massage, Movements—Creating a Sense of Communalism	Becoming more conscious that we are energy beings with an inner divinity. Energy is stimulated and energy blocks dissolved.	–Massage –Tai Chi –Yoga
Step 7: We Open Ourselves to the Experience of God, which Is Meditation	Overcoming the rational mind to open energy chakras where the inner divinity unites with God transcendent.	–Guided Breathing –Chanting –Guided Meditation –Love Circle –Prayer of Benediction

Concurrently, I summoned the Order of Nehemiah to install three shelves on the walls of each Mtoto House unit. These were to hold small, white, glass candles. Cardinal Nandi and I shopped for square tables to serve as the actual altar. We selected a red, a black, and a green twelve-inch candle and tall gold candleholders. Chimes, a crucifix, and a Bible were the finishing touches. All were placed on the altar table. We traveled to department stores and dance specialty shops to purchase shorts and leotards. Finally, all the items needed were acquired. Now, the actual training of houseparents was underway.

In our youth ministry meetings, we discussed the seven steps. However, for the cause of commonality, I committed myself to developing the entire devotional. What a daunting task! Initially, three devotionals were held each week! Sometimes, I could complete it in one night. Other times, I developed them while the children were in a two-hour sports session during summer camp. I can still hear their cheerful voices as I sat in the Training Center office, leafing through scriptures, reviewing awareness exercises, brainstorming activities for the discourse, composing the discourse, typing it all up, and making copies for ten houseparents.

Somehow, by sheer determination, I completed three typed devotionals a week for eight weeks. Each houseparent led it for their specific youth group. After the initial launching of devotionals, I trained houseparents to write them. Through discomfort and uncertainty, they tried.

They would explain and question.

"Cardinal Monifa, I am stuck. I don't know what to do next!"

"What awareness exercise should I choose?"

"Can you type it up for me?"

However, we were successful in creating approximately 200 typewritten devotionals.

After the pioneering experience with the children, Jaramogi summoned the leaders and potential facilitators from all regions to meet in Atlanta for national training on the KUA Group Devotionals. They would be held once a week for the adult membership. Their attire would be all white. KUA practitioners had the responsibility of implementing devotionals in their specific regions.

In Houston, we were advantaged to have devotionals in the Karamu Group House, a small mansion composed of at least ten rooms. What a beautiful edifice! Orange red brick adorned its outer beauty. Red carpet, elegant altars, a large, oil-painted portrait of Jaramogi, his father's medical certificate, memoirs of his parents and family ornamented its inner exquisiteness. Cardinal Nandi had an eye for interior decorating, so she and I visited trade markets to select furniture, altar items, and various portraits of the Black Madonna. I had the honor of naming each room, which included the Pearl Cleage Room, Dr. Albert B. Cleage Senior, Ola Mwanza, and Cardinal Nandi.

Houston was the urban enclave prototype. All institutions were within walking distance. Each Wednesday, members living in the three residence halls promenaded down Martin Luther King Boulevard in all white attire. Other members drove and parked either in the Cultural Center parking lot or on the U-shaped driveway. For those outside observers, I can only imagine what they thought as they beheld approximately 200 people dressed in white. For us, it was divinely mystical.

One day, Jaramogi softly mentioned to me, "Monifa, KUA Group Devotionals is our greatest contribution to Christianity."

He was steadfast in his quest to create a lifestyle that transforms people. I equate it with the following scripture: *"Truly, truly, I say to you, the one believing in Me, the works that I do, also he will do. And he will do greater than these, because I am going to the Father"* (John 14:12, BLB).

So, the science of KUA became an institutional process to consistently involve us in spiritual growth and spiritual intelligence.

Psychologist Robert Emmons defines spiritual intelligence as "the adaptive use of spiritual information to facilitate everyday problem solving and goal attainment." He originally proposed five components of spiritual intelligence.

- The capacity to transcend the physical and material.
- The ability to experience heightened states of consciousness.
- The ability to sanctify everyday experience.
- The ability to utilize spiritual resources to solve problems.
- The capacity to be virtuous.

I pondered. How many sleepless nights did Jaramogi experience? Was he able to look into the future and see a freed people? What gave him the faith to unrelenting pursue the well-being of Black people?

KUA Workshops

KUA workshops were instituted as one of the practices to self-realization. For the leadership and membership in Houston, we had the benefits of face-to-face meetings with Jaramogi in the development of the workshops. This was a three-hour experience.

Dressed in all white, members assembled in the Chapel of the Black Messiah, a special, red-carpeted room located inside the Cultural Center. I had the responsibility of preparing it. Strategically placing candles on the golden-brown armoires, lighting incense, and selecting gospel and meditation music were done intentionally. This ambience assisted members to reset their busy minds by entering a mystical sacred place. Upon entering, they were guided to sit in a circle.

The opening of the KUA workshop began with a facilitator pacing out the Sacred Circle. With chimes in hand, sweetly resonating, stepping in a slow gait outside of the circle, and chanting, "We step into the Sacred Circle where the power of God is," the facilitator began the journey of quieting minds while at the same time acknowledging the presence of God. The prayer of invocation followed as all stood with hands outstretched. We then lifted our voices in chants to erode any ego barrier that separated us in order to make us more susceptible to the God experience.

Tai chi followed. This was led by Molikai. We were upright in long rows that stretched from one wall to the other. He began. The slow rhythmic movements realigned our energy flow. Marvelously, as we glided into each posture in unison, a veil of peace hovered over the room. I embraced that experience of oneness!

After an hour of Tai chi, Molikai brought it to a smooth ending. I instructed members to quietly walk to a second room set up with chairs and a blackboard. After filing in and all of us seated, Jaramogi started a discourse lecture. The purpose was to increase our intellectual understanding of transformation.

In one session, Jaramogi lectured about our layers of identification; the Four Yous. Drawing four circles inside the other, he described the Four Yous.

1. The Visible You—what we want the world to see, our fronts.

2. The Secret You—the fears, guilts, and weaknesses that we keep private.

3. The Unconscious You—the part of us we are unaware of, but it still motivates our behaviors.

4. The Real You—the God within, the inner power.

These discourses linked mind development to spiritual growth. Each opened our minds. After his lecture, we returned to the Chapel of the Black Messiah.

The last hour of the workshop was designed for yoga and meditation. I instructed and guided members through the Sun Salutation, the Triangle, the Cobra, the Plow, the Shoulder Stand, the Warrior Pose, and the Lotus. When the actual movements were completed, each person lay on their backs.

Using visualization, I spoke. "Go to your feet. Tell your feet to relax. Relax. Relax. Now go to your legs. Tell your legs to relax. Relax. Relax."

We traveled from the toes to the top of the head, relaxing every part of the body. By the time we were at the chest, soft snoring silhouetted the room. Usually after twenty minutes of meditation, I spoke again. "When you hear the chimes, slowly open your eyes and slowly sit up." The benediction was given. With meditation music quietly playing, relaxed individuals floated out of the room. Certainly, these processes were lifechanging!

KUA Healing Ritual

The church must be able to heal based on the theological foundation that God is Cosmic Energy and Creative Intelligence and based on the belief that we too are energy beings. When we are open, a free flow of energy permeates each living cell and organ, restoring the body to health. Thus, healing is one of the practices of KUA based on the life of Jesus.

> *"While the sun was setting, all those who had any who were sick with various diseases brought them to Him, and laying His hands on each of them, He was healing them"* (Luke 4:40, NASB).

Jaramogi's mode of operation was to first discuss the healing aspect of KUA, utilizing the biblical healings in the Bible as evidence, specifically the healing power of Jesus. He was extremely serious about the church being able to do what Jesus did. As he discussed the importance of the healing ritual, he explicitly stated that those who wanted to be healed must have faith. Then, he asked me to organize it.

First, an announcement was placed in the Sunday's bulletin of the date and the time for the healing ritual. Members were invited to submit their names. During this interim, I met with four women ministers, KUA practitioners, to discuss and prepare for the healing ritual. We would fast the week before. We would all be dressed in white, flowing gowns. We would pray each day to be open vessels. We decided on the time to prepare the space for healing. We accepted our assigned duties.

The day of the healing ritual arrived. The holy space was the Chapel of the Black Messiah. We blessed the room and lit candles and incense. Soothing meditation music played over the sound system. The healing cot was placed in its location. It was handcrafted with a solid wooden oak base. On top of the base was a full-size cushion covered in red satin. The ministers prayed. All the preparation was completed.

Then those who requested healing were guided into the chapel. They were dressed in white. Each sat on a large, red, rectangular pillow as they silently prayed. One minister paced out the Sacred Circle while ringing chimes. The prayer of invocation was lifted.

I approached the first person and asked, "Do you have faith?"

"Yes, I have faith," he replied.

He was led to the healing cot and instructed to lay on his back with his arms at his sides. Amina, another minister accompanied me. We both clapped our hands, rubbed them together, and rotated them, palms down above his body seven times.

Then, I laid my hands on the Base Chakra—First Chakra.

Amina began to read.

The First KUA Affirmation. "Like every child growing up in the Black Nation Israel, Jesus was taught the Covenant, the Law, and the Prophets."

I repeated: "Like Jesus, we accept the Covenant, the Law, and the Prophets as revelations of God, binding upon His chosen people."

I laid my hands on the Sacral Chakra—Second Chakra.

Amina read.

The Second KUA Affirmation. The Quest. "Jesus sought the experience of God when he left Nazareth and walked the dangerous Jericho Road to Jerusalem to be baptized in the Jordan River where he heard the voice of God declare him to be the Messiah and a dove lighting upon his shoulder symbolized the fact that he had received the Holy Spirit."

I repeated: "Like Jesus, we too seek the experience of God. Kutafuta—Kutamungu Kugasana—Kujitoa."

We Seek the Experience of God

(Amina spoke the words of the Leader. I responded.)

Leader: **Kutafuta** means that we have entered the Sacred Circle and we seek the experience of God.

Response: We open ourselves to receive the power of God.

Leader: **Kutamungu** means that we can come upon God here where we are.

Response: If we seek, we will find.

Leader: When we are open, our inner divinity can be touched by the cosmic power of God and **Kugasana** will come like a mystical explosion.

Response: The overwhelming power of God enters into us, the Creative Intelligence of God directs us. We become one with God and with our people everywhere.

Leader: When our inner divinity comes into contact with the Higher Power, out of which it was created, we are born again in the fullness of life.

Response: The sacred triangles, the mystical sacraments, and the disciplines of the transforming community open us to receive the power of God.

Leader: In our surrender to God, **Kujitoa**, we have new strength for our earthly battles.

Response: We share a sacred trust with those who have gone before and with those who will come after. We are in total submission to the will of God. **Kujitoa.**

Kutafuta—Kutamungu—Kugasana—Kujitoa

I laid my hands on the Solar Plexus—Third Chakra.

Amina read.

The Third KUA Affirmation. The Renunciation. "Following his baptism, Jesus went into the wilderness where he fasted and prayed for forty days and forty nights. He was tempted by Satan who offered him all of the glories of the world to turn his back upon

God. Jesus rejected the temptations of Satan and renounced the slave culture by which Satan sought to tempt him."

I repeated: "Like Jesus, we too renounce Satan and all his ways. We renounce the slave culture, which tempts us with materialism, sensualism, and escapism. We place God first in our lives."

I laid my hands on the Heart Chakra—Fourth Chakra.

Amina read.

The Fourth KUA Affirmation. The Power. "Jesus with power of the Spirit, returned to Galilee and his reputation spread throughout the countryside. He taught in their synagogues, and everyone praised him. He taught, preached, and healed."

I repeated: "Like Jesus, the power of the Holy Spirit is available to us. We too have the power to teach, preach, and heal."

Amina continued: "In Matthew 21:22 [ESV], 'And whatever you ask in prayer, you will receive, if you have faith.'"

I laid my hands the Throat Chakra—Fifth Chakra.

Amina read.

The Fifth KUA Affirmation. The Fellowship. *"Jesus went up on a mountainside and called to him those he wanted, and they came to him. He appointed twelve that they might be with him and that he might send them out to preach and to have authority to drive out demons"* (Mark 3:13–15, NIV).

"His mother and brothers were standing outside and sent in a message. Jesus replied, *'Who are my mother and my brothers?' he asked. Then he looked at those seated in a circle around him and said, 'Here are my mother and my brothers! Whoever does God's will is my brother and sister and mother'"* (Mark 3:33–35, NIV).

I repeated: "Like Jesus, we recognize those associated with us in the task of building God's kingdom on earth as our family, and we have no other."

I laid my hands on the Aina Chakra—Sixth Chakra.

Amina read.

The Sixth KUA Affirmation. The Betrayal. "In the Garden of Gethsemane, Jesus was betrayed by all of his disciples. We see how easily the disciples betrayed Jesus when they lost faith and began to doubt."

I repeated: "We will not betray the sacred community upon which we depend for both our salvation and our survival.

I laid my hands on the Crown Chakra—Seventh Chakra.

Amina read.

The Seventh KUA Affirmation. The Incarnation. "According to the gospel of Mark, Jesus was anointed Messiah at the time of his baptism. After their betrayal and flight, the disciples came back together for prayer and meditation. They became the Messianic Community when they were touched by the Holy Spirit at Pentecost."

I repeated: "Today, we accept this church as the Messianic Community with the mission and power that Jesus had during his lifetime. Everything which Jesus did, we can do."

He lay there for a few minutes. Then he was led back to the circle with the red pillows. The laying on of hands continued until all seven were healed. They testified afterward.

"I experienced bliss and lightness," a middle-age man said.

"I had stage-four cancer," were the words spoken by a forty-year-old female.

"My kidneys were failing," a mother of two shared.

Still alive after twenty years, they believed that the healing ritual helped them.

Jaramogi wrote the KUA affirmations under the direction of the Holy Spirit and the experiences lived by Jesus. He was always planting the seeds of knowledge about Jesus' mission to teach, preach, and heal.

The BCN Message and Mission

I had the honor and privilege of assisting Jaramogi in sharing his brilliant tenets with the world. He wrote the BCN Message and Mission in 1987 as a culmination of his teachings. That year, the Bishops' Council in Houston decided to host a tribute for him in coordination with the tenth anniversary of Shrine Ten. I was assigned to organize the tribute.

As always, he felt that a souvenir booklet was necessary. It would include the position, philosophy, and spiritual foundations of his life's work. So, in addition to organizing the details of the tribute that included garnering the region to distribute leaflets, contacting radio stations for public service announcements, and inviting political officials, I was responsible for the development and completion of the souvenir booklet.

He gave me pages and pages of yellow tablet paper filled with his handwritten notes. I can still hear his words today.

"Monifa, this tribute and souvenir booklet is an albatross around your neck."

I had no idea what that was! Rushing to my dictionary, I anxiously looked up the meaning of albatross. Metaphorically it is an annoying burden, but literally it is a large sea bird. So, he meant it as an annoying burden.

I made several trips to the publisher, even at night, and brought the drafts back to him. Reviewing them closely, he suggested changes. At the same time, he trained me.

"Look in magazines. Notice how they use formatting, pictures, and font styles to create an engaging article," he advised.

I shared my newfound knowledge with the publisher.

Then during our next meeting, Jaramogi shared another valuable lesson.

"Monifa," he said in a serious tone, "the number of people who attend this tribute sends a message."

The implication was very clear. The number of people would be a direct reflection of his influence and work. That motivated me to use each ounce of organizational energy to make sure the tribute was well attended. It was!

On the Sunday of the tribute, 1,200 people packed the church. As I sat on the podium, he walked across from where he was sitting with a look of satisfaction on his face.

"Monifa, you did it," he said.

I smiled. I also knew that the concerted effort of my brothers and sisters in Houston made it happen!

The *BCN Message and Mission* is an evolution of Black Christian Nationalism. It is the sound theological framework that took several years to develop. I am proud that I played a major role in developing and editing that souvenir booklet.

In it, Jaramogi encapsulated the psychological trauma and conditioning of Black people in the context of our reality. He further describes how the life of Jesus is incorporated in the church, the fellowship of believers. *"In doing this, the Community of Jesus serves as viable actions for internal transformation that directly empowers us to change our external wretched conditions"* (Cleage).

IX

The Community of Jesus

"Jesus' ministry was based upon the history and the Messianic tradition of the Black Nation Israel, not the otherworldly Christ figure put together by the Apostle Paul and adopted by the Catholic Church. The Messiah anticipated by the Black Nation Israel had a political mission—social transformation, the origin of which was God. The process for the fulfillment of that mission required that people must be changed themselves before their collective condition as a people could be changed" (Jaramogi).

FOR THREE DECADES, THE THEOLOGY AND PRACTICES OF THE CHURCH evolved. The Central Region, Southern Region, and Southwest Region were established as the community of Jesus. This definition is not passive. It is a revolutionary active one. A community of people so changed that they can change the world.

"People change as a result of a group process. It is the constant pressure and love of a community committed to change that transforms people. Jesus' main goal was to build a Messianic Community—a community of people so changed that God could act through them to transform their condition and the world" (Jaramogi).

The group process was originally established as the process of transformation and continues to this day. This practice was evident in that all members were assigned to a group, which held them accountable to their commitment. Persons of like minds professed their belief in the liberation struggle, contributed financially, willingly accepted assignments and relocations, and dedicated loyalty and service to the group to which they were assigned.

Because of the group process, the church was able to expand rapidly and the institutions, over thirty properties, were centers that allowed for a counterculture. The communal dining rooms, nurseries, meditation centers, residence halls, cultural centers, and training centers helped to create a life that represented the love of Jesus and his revolutionary nature.

"Jesus concentrated his efforts on the immediate task of his messiahship, because the new world order of the Messianic Age could not be achieved by the Messiah alone. It could only come into effect through the agency of a Messianic Nation, all of whose members would know God, from the greatest of them to the least of them. The Messiah would be the redeemer of Israel and Israel would be the redeemer of mankind"(Schonfield, 1975).

The community of Jesus is based on the life, the teachings, and the love exhibited by the Messiah. This love is the synthesis that not only restores Black people to a life of freedom and justice but is the impetus that changes humankind. The selfishness, predatorial, evil intent of humankind is an antithesis to the community of Jesus.

"The Community of Jesus was built upon the foundation of revolutionary love, not the possessive, ego driven, emotionally draining concept of love that we have accepted. Revolutionary love for Jesus began with the Covenant and the Law. The Covenant was God's guarantee that we will triumph over the forces that restrict and burden us as a people. The Law stated the conditions we must meet to ensure our triumph as God's people" (Jaramogi).

There are three basic components to revolutionary love.

1. **Compassion.** There must be compassion on the part of one for another.

2. **Service.** There must be service. You must give totally of yourself to the accomplishment of goals that transcend your selfish desires and serve the interest of the group of which you are a part. Service demands that we sacrifice and invest all that we have in the movement.

3. **Awareness of Reality.** There must be a constant awareness of reality. Once you understand the nature of our social conditions as a people, your need for other people becomes obvious. When you realize that you need other people, you will

become more conscious of how you treat them. Human relationships become more important and precious as you recognize your need for community.

The community of Jesus, the Messianic Community, helps decrease the feeling of separation and alienation that plague people to perpetrate evil and violent acts against one another. The community provides a sense of purpose and belonging; thus, fulfilling emotional and social needs creates a healthier mental state. It also is the most productive environment for an overarching commitment of a group to build a better life for all.

I believed this and lived it. For three decades, Jaramogi's wisdom as my spiritual guide, revolutionary father, and entrusted leader nurtured and groomed me into becoming an empowered leader. Thanks to his teachings, I rose through the ranks, starting as a group leader of children and adult groups, then progressing to become an administrator at Shrine Two, a KUA practitioner, a Bible class lecturer, creator of rituals, writer of children's meditation stories specifically for summer camps, houseparent of children's groups who resided in Mtoto House—The Children's Institution, local and national youth coordinator, communal budget director, and an ordained bishop and cardinal. All of my life from twenty-one years old through my mid-fifties, from young through middle-age, I was dedicated to the Shrine of the Black Madonna.

Even in the last years of his life, he thought of a time that he would no longer be on earth. I was attending a ministers' meeting in his apartment at the Houston Missionary Institute and Training Center. As always, I stayed after to wash dishes and tidy up his place, because my mother's words lingered in my head very often.

"Shelley, you should always leave a place better than you found it," my mother always said.

And so, with Jaramogi, I felt it was my responsibility to do so. He was now in his eighties. As I was about to leave, he stopped me.

"Monifa, I want you to get your doctoral degree," he told me, with a concerned expression. "I don't know what niggas are going to do when I am gone."

Those words motivated me to sit at my computer in the wee hours of the morning researching, typing, and editing my dissertation. I did earn my doctorate of education degree in curriculum and instruction in 2002, two years after his death.

When I was fifty years old, Jaramogi died on Beulah Land. It was on Sunday, February 20, 2000. I was taking care of my husband, Awznee, who wasn't feeling well. So, I arrived at the church very late. As I headed for a parking space in the rear, I glanced at members exiting the sanctuary. Something was different about them. They were walking slowly with sullen faces. That image quickly left my mind as I found a place to park. Stepping out of the car, I walked alongside the Training Center toward the door. Lieutenant Sundiata, a six-foot-four Maccabee, walked toward me.

"Hi, how are you doing?" I greeted him.

He looked down at me. "You must not know," he said.

"Know what?" I asked.

"Jaramogi died."

I slumped over as if a mighty wind had pounded my abdomen, gust after gust. From deep within, a bellowing painful cry rose up and tears flooded my face. I was too shocked and too weak to take another step. Sundiata had to almost carry me into the building where he set me down in a chair as I still cried uncontrollably. The founder, spiritual leader, and creator of Black Christian Nationalism, Jaramogi Abebe Agyeman, was gone.

From that cold day in January 1971 when I joined, until the sunny, hot day in Houston in 2000, almost thirty years, I'd trusted Jaramogi's leadership. Within the safety and security of the church community, I developed Mtoto House and was its director for twenty-one years. The mission was to nurture our children socially, spiritually, academically, and physically. I organized morning rituals, afterschool programs, eight-week summer camp programs, and religious observations.

Children were taught African history and received the factual interpretation about the Bible and Jesus. They experienced yoga and meditation and were taught to read before kindergarten. We enhanced their reading skills while they matriculated through school, and academically supported them to successfully graduate from high school. Without monetary rewards, I was driven by the dream of freedom spearheaded by Jaramogi. I believed. I was totally committed.

I Give You a Mustard Seed

It has been at least two decades since Jaramogi's death, but BCN still is a foundation for liberation. Much has changed since his passing. The number of institutions acquired through the blood, sweat, and tears of members has decreased significantly. Because of that, the internal infrastructure itself was affected, lessening the number of spaces used for communal dining, nurseries, residence halls, training centers, Mtoto Houses, and KUA Meditation Centers.

The domino effect created a downturn in the consistent practices of disciplines and rituals, which were designed to open individuals to community and to the experience of God. However, what cannot be denied is that Black Christian Nationalists had become one people and proved to ourselves that we could change our behaviors, expand to three regions, and create sacred kinship bonds. What we had not yet become was a Nation with power.

This was the challenge after his death. Although our properties and institutions were tangible products of our commitment, what would be the next steps in maintaining them and building power?

I pondered these questions in my heart and mind, day and night: "What can we show for our sacrifices? What stories do we tell our children? Was it all in vain? Do we die of this life leaving only a shadow of evidence of our work?"

Jaramogi often was stark and piercing in his comments. "We may be the only people who never got free," he said. "Get your own faith. You are riding off of the faith of those in the civil rights movement," he admonished. "Once you gain power, it is harder to maintain it," he wisely taught. "We're on a downward spiral," he lamented one day.

That stunned me! Why would he say that? Like many others, I had given everything. Hundreds of us believed in the possibility of being free from oppression and exploitation. I felt pain hearing those words coming from him. But with deep contemplation, I caught a glimpse of what he meant.

"I give you a mustard seed by which you can move mountains if you have a mind to," Jaramogi announced to the church's membership.

The mustard seed mentioned in the scriptures and by Jaramogi grows into a mustard tree. These trees grow wildly throughout the Middle East and Africa. Germinating in phases, small sprouts emerge from underneath the soil. Eventually, the trees reach a height no taller than twenty-five feet, being nurtured by the earth's soil and water and by the rays of the sun. The mustard seed is already engrained by God to evolve. It only needs an environment to do so.

For me, the mustard seed that Jaramogi gave to us is best illustrated in Table 4.

Table 4: The Mustard Seed

Committed Leadership

Exemplified in teachings, actions, love, and determination to share the vision, while concurrently supporting people and meeting their physical and developmental needs.

Awareness of Reality

We are Black. We are oppressed. We seek to end our oppression.

Theological Foundation

We seek to establish and maintain a covenant relationship with God.
We acknowledge that Jesus was a Black Messiah. His life teaches us that nothing is more sacred than the liberation of Black people.

Program and Projection

We organize on the basis of creating self-determination for all Black people. The vision and goals are explicitly stated and taught.

Transforming Community

Changing the minds of Black people is intentional and critical for a lifelong commitment. Change occurs in the Messianic Community through socialization.
Experience of God.
Experience of Community.
Experience of Communalism.

Jaramogi Abebe Agyeman was totally committed. Organizing the BCN program, defining ways of behaviors, training and creating an environment for transformation was an all-consuming life endeavor. All that he required us to do in practicing communalism, he did. He lived in the residence halls, wore the same uniforms, ate meals in the communal dining rooms, and attended orientations and worship services.

He identified gifts and talents of individuals, assigning some to run for political office and others to assume leadership positions in the church. He mentored and criticized simultaneously and projected goals that were actually achieved. He was compassionate. Because of his example, I totally committed myself to the work of the church, to the liberation of my people as I understood it. I believed in him.

Jaramogi lived what he believed.

Living the Vision of Liberation

As with many others, I actually lived the life in a communal, self-sustaining Black community. Not always perfect but tied to a common mission and belief. Even through challenges and differences, the vision of a better world created a sacred bond.

We built and experienced a community that was drug-free, debt-free, no murders, no hunger, and no housing insecurities. Individuals voluntarily committed themselves to a higher cause, a greater calling. I actually experienced a spiritual oneness with my brothers and sisters.

My faith was in the works of the Black Messiah, Jesus, in the power of his disciples, and in the revelations of the prophets. As with my adult peers, I possessed an undying love for our children and hope for their futures.

I sought enlightenment and discovered the path of self-knowledge to know the greatness of our true Black selves. It was a nonviolent, nonmilitant approach for social justice through creating our own institutions for self-determination. In controlling our institutions, we change our communities and exist peacefully as a Nation within the wider US community as other racial and religious groups do.

So, the contribution of Black Christian Nationalists, the living legacies and those who have gone on before, was to be an example of possibility. To dare take a giant leap with hopes of creating a nation, a kingdom of God on earth, may serve to be an inspiration to many.

Unlike the mustard seed whose DNA is programmed for evolvement, for Black Christian Nationalists and even for the Black Church, it is conditional. They must have a mind to.

The Black Church—Will It Mobilize People to Build Power Collectively?

I have experienced and learned that building institutions, that building power, are undergirded by the human value of revolutionary love. Compassion, service, and an awareness of reality are components of this love. Only the conscious rejection of individualism can open individuals to living and expressing revolutionary love. Without it, organizations fade or simply blend in with the norms of the world system, offering no viable program for liberation.

To mobilize takes committed and effective leadership. Membership of churches includes politicians, teachers, military men and women, school administrators, teachers, business owners, fraternities and sororities, public servants, athletes, and politicians. Hundreds of Black people are engaged in activities that support and nurture, such as, Black farmers, community organizations, and celebrities. We need unity for one goal: to end our oppression.

Because of the leadership of Jaramogi Abebe Agyeman, a prototype to mobilize Black people actually existed. To sustain and expand it to supersede his death depended on "if you have a mind to." This rested on the shoulders of the new leadership.

For the living Black Christian Nationalists who sacrificed all of their young lives for the expansion and sustainability of the church, pain grips many of our hearts. We gave up careers, jobs, and educational pursuits for the dream of freedom. Our leader was our example. Now, our institutions are gone! Our promise to our children of a better world, broken! Our belief that they would inherit a nation, shattered! Our value, devalued!

Leadership is everything! "If you have a mind to," serves as a self-reflection and honest evaluation of one's own motives and actions. To build on what was established under the leadership of Jaramogi Abebe Agyeman, the following is critical.

1. Leader—Committed to communalism and the vision of freedom.

2. Leadership Core—Committed to the welfare, health, happiness, training, and prosperity of all its membership.

3. Embracing the Gifts of Young People—Provide space and opportunities for their voices, talents, education, and organizational skills, channeling their energies to grow into leadership.

4. Building Relationships—Reaching out to like-minded church leaders to share resources, monies, talents, and to build institutions.

5. Reinvest in Institutions—There is an answer to everything if the goal is to sustain institutions. Collaborative thinking, being open to ideas, and accepting those ideas. For example: When the training center and residence halls were being sold, young people were willing to collectively donate to save them.

6. Expansion—Projections to expand to other cities.

7. Recruitment—Continuous efforts to bring in others.

8. Messianic Communities—Self-sustaining communities that not only transform people through a group process but also provide a network to exchange goods and services.

9. Sustain Core of Full-Time People.

10. Love for Black people.

We must be unified in a common belief, philosophy, and program to create Messianic communities everywhere. What Black Christian Nationalists have done can be done again! Seeds have been planted in our children and sown throughout the land. Jaramogi Abebe Agyeman once said, "If there is one Black Christian Nationalist left, he or she will rebuild Black Christian Nationalism."

Just perhaps, generations now and generations yet to come will germinate the seeds of liberation and freedom will come!

Appendices

The appendices include actual documents and writings of Reverend Albert B. Cleage Jr. (Jaramogi Abebe Agyeman). These are on file at the University of Michigan, Bentley Historical Library. The author contacted the library and was informed that these were donated by the Cleage family with no copyrights. The documents provide complete explanations and BCN teachings.

      Appendix A—BCN Message and Mission
      Appendix B—Poetry by Jaramogi
      Appendix C—BCN Covenant
      Appendix D—BCN Statement of Faith
      Appendix E—BCN Code
      Appendix F—BCN Program
      Appendix G—BCN Teaches
      Appendix H—BCN Position
      Appendix I—BCN Goals at Basic Training Levels
      Appendix J—BCN Basic Training Pledge

APPENDIX A
BCN Message and Mission
Revolutionary Transformation
1987
Introduction

Jesus' ministry was based upon the history and the Messianic tradition of the Black Nation Israel, not the otherworldly Christ figure put together by the Apostle Paul and adopted by the Catholic Church. The Messiah anticipated by the Black Nation Israel had a political mission (social transformation), the origin of which was God. The process for the fulfillment of that mission required that people must be changed themselves before their collective condition as a people could be changed.

Up to the period just preceding the beginning of Jesus' ministry those who were called to act for God in the interest of the Black Nation Israel assumed that man was a rational information processing organism. But beginning with the Essenic movement and the Community at Qumran approximately 150 B.C.) a new notion arose that individuals must be brought into an environment structured to change people.

People change as a result of a group process. It is the constant pressure and love of a community committed to change that transforms people.

Jesus' main goal was to build a Messianic Community—a community of people so changed that God could act through them to transform their condition and the world.

> *"Jesus concentrated his efforts on the immediate task of his messiahship because the new world order of the Messianic age could not be achieved by the Messiah alone. It could only come into effect through the agency of a Messianic Nation, all of who members would know God, from the greatest of them to the least of them. The Messiah would be the redeemer of Israel and Israel would be the redeemer of mankind."* —For Christ Sake, Schonfield 1975

The Community of Jesus was built upon the foundation of revolutionary love— not the possessive, ego driven, emotionally draining concept of love that we have accepted. Revolutionary love for Jesus began with the covenant and the law.

The **Covenant** was **God's guarantee** that we will triumph over the forces that restrict and burden us as a people.

The **Law** stated the **conditions** we must meet to ensure our triumph as God's people. *"I have not come to abolish the Law and the prophets but to fulfill them."* (Matthew 5:17)

To make of the Law and the prophets a foundation for revolutionary love, Jesus taught his followers in the Sermon on the Mount to look at the Law not as simply policies to be followed arbitrarily but with concern for how they affected the relationships between people. Jesus' expectations for behavior and relationships went far beyond what most people assumed was normal. *"For, I tell you, unless your righteousness exceeds that of the Pharisees, you will never enter the Kingdom of heaven."* (Matthew 5:20)

There are Three Basic Components to Revolutionary Love

- There must be *compassion* on the part of one for another." *If you are offering your gift at the altar and there remember that your brother has something against you, leave your gift there before the altar and go; first be reconciled to your brother, and then come and offer your gift."* Matthew 5:23-24

  Try to work out the problems that have hurt your relationship with your brother or sister. Do not avoid the interpersonal conflicts or act as if they do not exist. But Jesus did not preach a mindless unconditional compassion to his followers. *"If your brother sins, rebuke him; if he repents, forgive him. If he sins against you seven times in a day and turns to you seven times and says, I repent, you must forgive him."* Luke 17: 3-4

  People are not perfect. They don't always do what they should, but when they sin (violate the Law), you should confront them. If they are truly sorry for their sin, you should forgive them. Jesus says in Matthew 18: *"If a brother rejects the authority of the church/Black Nation, then let him be to you as a gentile and tax collector."*

  A Messianic Community exists to save people—to help them become a more effective part of the life and mission of a revolutionary movement.

- There must be *service*. You must give totally of yourself to the accomplishment of goals that transcend your selfish desires and serve the interest of the group of which you are a part. *"If any man would come after me, let him deny himself, and pick up his cross and follow me."* Mark 8: 34 *"But whoever would be great among* you must be your servant." Mark 20:26 *"The son of man came not to be served but to serve."* (Mark 10: 34) Service demands that we sacrifice and invest all that we have in the movement.

- There must be a constant *awareness of reality*. Once you understand the nature of our social condition as a people, your need for other people becomes obvious. When you realize that you need other people, you will become more conscious of how you treat them. Human relationships become more important and precious as you recognize your need for community. Personal romantic relationships and nuclear families are much too fragile a foundation upon which to stake your whole sense of worth and value. Your life, if it is to have any real hope, security, and meaning, must be tied to a reality that completely transcends your existence as an individual. *"But he said to them my mother and my brothers are those who hear the word of God and do it."* (Luke 8: 21)

While most churches are content to prepare members for the experience of death, we teach our members the healing rituals which restore health to body and mind, making it possible to achieve the Experience of God and the joy of an abundant life. *Kujitoa,* submission to the will of God, and the acceptance of Divine Obligations, makes all of life a revolutionary struggle for social change and a joyous celebration.

BCN Seeks to change slaves who suffer not only from a slave condition but also from a slave mentality.

During the past several years we have placed a major emphasis upon developing the theological and psychological foundations of the BCN Change Process. Beginning with the faith that salvation is a group process and the biblical account of Pentecost where the power of the Holy Spirit changed the disciples, we developed the BCN Change Process. This development is now complete.

During the same period we failed to keep our everyday training group practices abreast of our rapidly developing Change Theory. Our training groups and group activities were not actually changing members nor attracting new members who could see the results of our change process and recognize a need for the process in their own lives. In fact, few church leaders or members realize that the BCN Change Process is our reason for being and must be the basis of our Community Outreach Program. Our 1985 National Conclave re-established the BCN Change Process as our top national priority. This has served to revitalize our entire program (Sunday Service, Missionary Outreach, Community Outreach, Youth Programs, groups, etc.).

BCN seeks to change slave who suffer not only from a slave condition but also from a slave mentality. Everywhere in the world Black people are powerless, enslaved by a hostile society which has declared them inferior, and incapable of full participation as equals. Four hundred years of powerlessness and enslavement in a hostile exploitative society has had profound psychological effects upon Black people. We have been incapacitated for effective struggle against our condition by a basic acceptance of the Declaration of Black Inferiority. Our powerless condition has led us to create a slave culture (a sub-culture of the powerless) characterized by identification with our oppressor and a futile dream of escape through integration.

The slave culture dictates a time ritual, a value system, and a life style, and no slave can be liberated while he remains in the slave culture, has one foot in the slave culture, or still lusts after the irresponsibility of the slave culture.

BCN takes slaves out of the slave culture and substitutes a new BCN Time Ritual, a new BCN Value System, and a new BCN Life Style. Everything possible is done to heighten the distinction between the BCN Life Style and the slave culture life style. No compromise is permitted. No back-sliding is tolerated. No personal problems are accepted as legitimate excuses or justification for failure to make a clean break with the slave culture. We do not pretend that this is an easy or pleasant transformation. It can only be compared to the pain of withdrawal from dope. Withdrawal from the slave culture involves a total change in the mentality of a slave. It can only be accomplished with the help and support of a group which is concerned. Painful group criticism is a basic part of this process! Unwillingness to confront a slave when he tries to sneak back to the slave culture only serves to retard his withdrawal and indicates slave culture tendencies upon the part of those who only pretend to be participants in a group process! Without this BCN Group Process there can be no liberation of Black people any place in the world!

The Black Slave Mentality

The Black slave mentality is the result of operant conditioning, a familiar tool of experimental psychologist in which an animal or human is rewarded when he carries out a desired task or is punished for performing in an undesirable manner. Black people in America are victims of a systematic program of behavior modification utilizing operant conditioning and have been rendered incapable of rational action designed to change their condition.

With the loss of freedom to act, the victim has lost his identity. A victim of operant conditioning loses the ability to act in any way counter to his conditioning. (*A Clockwork Orange* by Anthony Burgess). He is a slave-controlled by his oppressors from within his own head. Mass communication media, public education, the Church, and industry offer negative reinforcement to the Black incapacity to act purposefully.

The basic human drive for status has been short-circuited by operant conditioning finding expression only in nonproductive, self-destructive behavior. This explains the failure of Black leaders, organizations, and undertakings which sought to change the Black man's condition without first changing his mind. Our conditioning began with the cultural shock and brutality of the slave trade and the plantation which together were responsible for the death of more than 100 million Black people.

The victims of the Black Holocaust included every African whether taken from his homeland in chains or left to witness the destruction of African civilization and the decimation of her people.

In a world which has accepted materialism, individualism, hedonism and the ruthless use of power as social norms, the Christian Church must give every man the answer which Jesus gave Nicodemus when he asked, "What must I do to be saved? You must be born again." In addition to the universal problem of human corruption and depravity, the Black Church faces an additional problem in that it must minister to the survival victims of a Black Holocaust which took the lives of one hundred million Africans during the American Slave Trade.

The Africans could not withstand the cultural shock of the slave experience in which millions were killed in the attacks upon helpless villages and in the barbaric transport in overcrowded slave ships to cruel conditioning farms in the islands designed to systematically break men in preparation for the plantation and the inhuman institution of chattel slavery established in America. The victims of the Black Holocaust included every African whether taken from his homeland in chains or left to witness the destruction of African civilization and the decimation of her people.

The victims were forced to live with a complete moral inversion in which every man's purpose was to be cruel and to inflict pain and make his victims feel worthless. He was forced to accept the oppressor's declaration of Black inferiority taught with a sophisticated system of operant conditioning involving constant physical and psychological torture. Everything the African had taken for granted and depended upon was suddenly snatched from him, homeland, language, religion and community. He was miserable and alone. Each day of torture brought new pain, new loneliness and a new hopelessness.

For Africans throughout the world, life became a horrifying experience and then a painful memory to be repressed and pushed down into the unconscious mind to control behavior as unconscious motivation. The psychological damage to the African is beyond comprehension. Not only was the enslaved generation rendered psychologically ill, the effects have been culturally transmitted from generation to generation down to the present. A mentally sick generation cannot but hand its sickness down to its children.

This is especially true of a slave experience which never ended. The torture of slavery continued in the torture of Reconstruction administered by the Ku Klux Klan and legitimatized and supported by the Black Codes and the government. The torture continued in the urban ghettos of the North where discrimination, police brutality, economic exploitation and exclusion from the main stream of American life constantly reinforced the psychological sickness suffered by the descendants of slaves. Poverty, crime, juvenile delinquency, the failure of schools to educate Black children, prisons, and mental hospitals jammed with young Black men continue the tortures of the African Slave Trade, and reinforce its continuing effects upon victims of the Black Holocaust.

For us the Experience of God is the basis of a revolutionary struggle for self-actualization and social change designed to transform our wretched Black condition here on earth.

People come into the Pan African Orthodox Christian Church seeking to end the wretchedness and loneliness of a Black condition grounded in the individualism of niggerization and characterized by:

- Isolation, empty personal relationships, and the absence of community.
- Poverty, which grows ever more threatening with our growing technological obsolescence.
- Ignorance, and the continuing failure of schools to educate Black children.
- Conditioned acceptance of inferiority with feelings of worthlessness and self-hatred.
- Patterns of escapism and negative belief systems.
- Inner conflict, frustration, and blind rage.

Our ability to meet these needs must be the basis of our community outreach and our Church program. Therefore, we must clearly articulate and implement a BCN Program of Revolutionary Transformation or we have no basis for community outreach nor can we hope to meet the needs of members who join urgently seeking this transformation.

We do not merely substitute a new spiritual mysticism based upon the experience of God for the old otherworldly escapism of the traditional Black Church based upon the blood redemption of Christ, and heaven in the sky after death. For us the experience of God is the basis of a revolutionary struggle for self-actualization and social change designed to transform our wretched Black condition here on earth. It is the basis for our commitment to the struggle. It is not an end in itself.

Black people must find healing in the fellowship and program of a Transforming Community.

The basis of revolutionary transformation is love, not power nor institutional strategy and tactics. The Pan African Orthodox Christian Church exists to change both the individual and the world in which he lives. We are a Transforming Community in which members may end the pain, hopelessness, and frustration of their wretchedness. As the woman with the issue of blood pushed her way through the crowd to touch the hem of Jesus' garment and find healing, Black people must find healing in the fellowship and program of a Transforming Community designed to help them remove blocks which prevent the experiencing of the group. Members must have the capacity to belong, to become a part of the community, to drop defenses and false fronts, to love freely and without restraint, to consider the needs of the group more important than their own.

The Church is a community of persons existing in a unified energy field which is God, voluntarily associated together because they share a common commitment to this supreme Power, out of which they have been created, and upon which they depend for the incarnate life force which is human life. God is one constantly expanding unified cosmic energy field combining the four fundamental forces of nature, in which we live, move, and have our being, and from which we derive life, meaning, values, and direction. The essence of all being is energy. The Church seeks to utilize this energy system upon which life depends by bringing together a fellowship of persons who practice the disciplines, rituals and sacraments which open the individual for both the experience of God and the experience of community.

Niggerization has led to our acceptance of the white man's declaration of Black inferiority, and has conditioned us to accept individualism as the cornerstone of our slave culture life style. Together these two negative forces prevent the practice of communalism which is essential to our survival. Our actions reflect the basic inner conflicts which keep us torn between contradictory positions in all areas of life. As Black people, we require assistance in the painful task of bringing these repressed conflicts up into consciousness where they can be confronted and resolved making possible the restoration of inner harmony and the essential integration of the Black personality. We are helpless without the disciplines of a structured communal group of which we are a part. In the Pan African Orthodox Christian Church, we call these disciplines KUA, the science of becoming that which God created us to be.

Only the total transformation of the Black man's mind can end Black oppression.

We must admit and confront the niggerization to which we have been subjected by our oppression. We will never free ourselves from oppression until each Flack person is willing to commit himself to self-transformation, rejecting his niggerized mind and its acceptance of the declaration of Black inferiority. All Black people need a transforming community with a process for self-transformation in which they can be changed. Neither politics, preachers nor drugs can save us. Only a process which can produce changed minds can end our oppression. The Black man's condition grows steadily worse with increasing unemployment, but we do not need militant speeches, protests, and marches. We need a practical process for changing the way Black people think.

Black Muslims once called the white oppressor a beast because of the way he acted. They developed the idea symbolically with the Yacub [sic] Myth and derogatory comments like, "He smells like a dog." Harsh environmental conditions warped and twisted the white man's mind. His behavior everywhere is characterized by individualism, sexism, and racism.

The white man's power results from his barbaric ruthlessness learned in a cold and barren Europe where he was forced to fight for his very existence. His struggle for food contributed to his brutalization. His need for land and resources led to conquest and a value system having little regard for human life. The white man used violence to attain domination and the wanton exploitation of everything to attain power. He had no appreciation for the world in which he lives, fouling earth, air, and water, and forcing his will upon less violent people by declaring them inferior, thus removing them from human consideration and preparing the way for a niggerization process of operant conditioning.

The Black man's basic oppression has been the conditioning of his mind and behavior to think and act like a white man, while excluded from the institutional power structure. The power centers of the economic system upon which society depends deny him the skills, knowledge, and technology ty which the white man maintains his power as well as the natural resources, the means of production, and full use of the international monetary system. All Black people, including "good niggers" and "professional negroes" are powerless, standing on the outside looking in at the white enemy system, unaware of the invisible barriers which hold them out and restrict them to second class citizenship as an "underclass." They think and act like white men without consciously realizing the demoralizing effect the niggerization process has had upon their minds and behavior.

Only the total transformation of the Black man's mind can end Black oppression. The Black man cannot be liberated. He must liberate himself by freeing his mind from the niggerization imposed by his white oppressor. To end his oppression, the Black man must change both his mind and his behavior. He must stop thinking and acting like a white man. He must reject his acceptance of the white man's declaration of Black inferiority and his slavish imitation of the white man's barbaric value system and life style which he has built into a slave culture. This essential self-transformation is much more difficult than attempting to punish the white man by physically attacking him and or his property with riots and ineffective attempts to use urban guerilla warfare.

All Black efforts to end oppression have reflected the Black man's faith in one or all of three futile approaches to his problem, and all have failed because they did not change the Black man's niggerized mind. His theoretical commitment to mass action has blinded him to the faulty analysis upon which his mass action organizations and programs have been founded. His blind faith in an all-powerful anthropomorphic God, watching over him has immobilized him for any serious effort to change his condition. Efforts at direct escape through the use of alcohol, addictive drugs, sex, religious emotionalism and otherworldly dreams of heaven somewhere in the sky has served to reduce all Black effort to impotence.

Self-help efforts to ameliorate the effects of oppression have also been undertaken by the Black man. Mutual assistance societies, church buying clubs, "Buy Black" campaigns to support Black businesses, lodges, credit unions, burial clubs, and small banks have sought to increase economic power by pooling the Black man's meager economic resources. They, too, failed because of their inability to secure substantial Black support. The Black man's niggerized mind is unable to conceive of the possibility of success for any Black enterprise. Only those Black undertakings offering service which the white man denies to Black people have had any chance of success!

Black people have never built a large effective mass-based organization. Black people resist organization because of their acceptance of Black inferiority. The masses are always dissatisfied, but do not trust Black leadership and are never really considered important by leadership.

Black organizations have never organized any significant number of Black people and never considered it necessary in that they only existed to touch the conscience of white people. Since the Emancipation Proclamation, Black organizations have had no program to change Black people's acceptance of the myth of Black inferiority. Slave insurrections were small and Reconstruction led to the re-enslavement of Blacks by the Ku Klux Klan. World War 1 began the northern migration of Blacks and a new urban industrial enslavement.

The Practice of KUA

"My little daughter lieth at the point of death; I pray Thee, come and lay thy hands on her that she may be healed, that she shall live." Mark 5:23

Three theses form the basis for our discussion of KUA.

Thesis 1—We clearly define the frustrations, tensions, deprivation and misery which constitute the Black condition and the world-wide injustices which are responsible. These world-wide dislocation contribute to the destruction of the Black man's spirit, mind, body integration creating energy blocks, repressions, illness and a critical need for therapy if Black people are to survive. We begin with niggerization which served as the theme of our Second Leadership Conclave of 1985.

Thesis 2—We clearly recognize the fact that the socialization of Black people, moving them from individualism to communalism using the group process to break down the walls of individualism and the Unified Energy Field to realign and reactivate the incarnate life-force for the Kugasana Experience and the attainment of a higher consciousness, make it possible for individuals to serve as conduits for God's power in healing and in the transformation of the world.

Thesis 3—The Practice of KUA offers a complete therapy for the "awakened group," utilizing meditation, movements, sacraments and rituals to provide a complete system of body, mind training designed to lead the group to the mystical spiritual "opening" which permits the incarnate life-force to be touched by the Cosmic Energy and Creative Intelligence of the Unified Cosmic Energy Field, which is God. The group is healed by the Kugasana Experience of God and receives the power to heal others and to bring the world, its governments and institutions into conformity with the will of God. The Seven KUA Affirmations in conjunction with the "Laying on of Hands," constitute the basic Healing Ritual of the Pan African Orthodox Christian Church (*Second Conclave Study Guide* 1986).

KUA offers a process by which the blocks caused by repression can be removed by the activation of the deepest levels of healing energy within ourselves and others.

The unwillingness to be opened so that love becomes the dominant element of the communal life of the Messianic Community prevents the three regions of the Pan African

Orthodox Christian Church from functioning effectively and reaching their highest potential. We are not effectively using the disciplines, rituals, sacraments and group processes because we refuse to renounce the individualism which is destroying Black people. The pain, hopelessness, and frustration of the Black condition cannot be changed unless those who seek change realize that they are in fact searching for a joyful existence with security, happiness, and meaning within a communal framework of honest personal relationships. Only through complete commitment and loyalty to the Pan African Orthodox Christian Church and total participation can an individual undertake to change his Black condition. This commitment and loyalty require a completely new understanding of God, Jesus, and Christian Fellowship.

God is the Cosmic Energy and Creative Intelligence out of which all things were created. We experience God in the fellowship of the church. The church is the Messianic Community in which God is incarnate and through which God has chosen to work in the world. The church then is more than a group of people professing faith in Jesus Christ as the redeeming son of God. The church is the living body of God possessing the power and ability to act for God in the world. Love of the members for each other and for the task of revolutionary transformation changes a group of individuals into a Messianic Community with the power to save.

The Pan African Orthodox Christian Church teaches that God is Cosmic Energy and Creative Intelligence. So, religion deals with energy and power. The life-force or incarnate divinity in each individual is the Divinity placed in man at the moment of creation. It flows along energy meridians and through the seven energy chakras unless blocked. Sickness occurs when the free flow of energy in the body is blocked.

Niggerization caused by an oppressor's operant conditioning leads to the acceptance of Black inferiority and then to its psychological repression because the individual cannot live with a conscious awareness of this conditioned acceptance. Although repressed, this acceptance of Black inferiority continues to function as unconscious motivation causing non-rational thinking and persistent non-adjustive behavior.

Repression, the forcing of a painful memory down into the unconscious mind, blocks the free flow of the fundamental life energy upon which the health of the individual depends.

KUA offers a process by which the blocks caused by repression can be removed by the activation of the deepest levels of healing energy within ourselves and others. This process depends upon the reality of the cosmos as it exists. All energy is unified in a single energy field (God). Everything in the universe is energy. Matter is compressed energy. We were created by God, out of the very substance of divinity and the spark of divinity in each of us if the life-force. Through KUA, we are able to realign and reactivate the energy in ourselves and others, thereby, healing by restoring the harmonious relationship with the cosmos intended by God.

When we consider changing individuals as we do in KUA, we are concerned with changing people from individualism to communalism. Basically, we are dealing with the problem of socialization. The individual is taught to conform to the behavioral norms of a group. We must learn to belong! This is the group experience! The group tears down the walls of individualism. Socialization is necessary before the individual can seek the experience of God! The group then is basic to the Practice of KUA. The individual resists belonging because he does not wish to sacrifice individualism! This is a paradox.

KUA is the science of becoming what we already are. We are created by God with the capacity to love and belong but from birth we are conditioned to be individualistic. We build up walls of individualism. Fear of others is learned. Fear, insecurity, and paranoia are learned at home. Children learn from their parents.

We must learn to belong.

Socialization is necessary before the individual can seek the experience of God. The Science of KUA must undertake the socialization of the individual before undertaking the spiritual preparation required for healing and the experience of God. Most people find it difficult if not impossible to seriously seek the experience of God because socialization has not been accomplished.

"How can you love God whom you have not seen, if you cannot love your brother with whom you live daily?"

We must learn to belong. We must learn to let our defenses down and depend upon the group or we cannot let down individualistic defenses and depend upon God. God has chosen to work through the group rather than the individual. A messiah was sent to the Black Nation Israel. The disciples at Pentecost were a group who became the church, the Messianic Community. Thus, the pscyho-social changes which are achieved by socialization affecting body/mind at the same time make possible the spiritual preparation of the individual to act as a conduit transmitting the power of God and to be opened for the experience of God-Kugasana. The group and the group experience are basic to the practice of KUA.

Rituals are designed to remove body/mind blocks by activating the inner life-force and re-establishing the free flow of inner energies, thereby, releasing repressed experiences and permitting them back up into consciousness and opening the individual for healing and the Pentecostal experience of God.

Opening occurs only when the energy level of the group is raised to the boiling point as though tongues of fire has come to rest over each head, and the group becomes an irresistible vortex of power, an energy center like a mighty tornado. Admit your wretched condition! Rituals then become positive action to open your life to God through the power of the Holy Spirit.

The Ritual of Invocation

Within the sacred circle, realizing that God is everywhere and will come into our lives when we are open, we seek to prepare ourselves for the worship experience. The sense of awe, mystery, unseen power and anticipation of the miraculous constitute an inescapable foundation, the Ritual of Invocation. I need Thee every hour. I need Thee.

The Ritual of Confession and Penance

Admit guilt, pain, and suffering. Admit repression. You do not know the cause of your pain. Renounce the slave culture and niggerization which enslave us and bind us in chains to our pain and frustration.

The Ritual of Purification

I come to the altar with no merit of my own . . . confessing my sins . . . knowing that I can do nothing to help myself. I throw myself upon the mercy of God. I would wash away my sins. Amazing grace how sweet the sound that saved a wretch like me.

The Ritual of Unity and Love

Lean on me. Touch me. Ritual of Blood Unity. I am one with my people everywhere.

Remembrance of ancestors through libation. We share a sacred trust with those who have gone on before and with those who will come after.

The Ritual of Healing

The laying on of hands.

The Ritual of Intercession

The morphogenetic energy fields. These are fields of thought created by everything in existence; it is the input and output of creation. We transmit the power of God.

The Ritual of Celebration

We acknowledge the power of God. We submit to the power. We confess our weakness. We seek power to overcome. Celebration of the Holy Spirit. Satan, I'm going to tear your kingdom down. I believe. Help my unbelief.

The group is basic to the practice of KUA, and the attainment of health, happiness, and prosperity. To reach our full potential, we must reject individualism by participating in a community of believers who accept a covenant relationship with God and a communal relationship with their brothers and sisters. God works through the group as the instrument of change.

- The Act of Belonging (Rejection of individualism)
- The Act of Internalizing the Law (Behavioral norms)
- The Practice of Communal Living
- The Acts of Confession and Confrontation (The group encounter)
- The Act of Loving One Another (Mandatum)
- To Experience the Opening (Makes possible the mystical union)
- The Act of Working (To bring the world into conformity with the will of God, involving both evangelical and revolutionary activity).

The group is the instrument of change utilizing KUA Processes.

Socialization is the basis of change. It is the acceptance of behavioral norms implicit in the acceptance of the Covenant and explicit in the acceptance of the Black Christian Nationalist Code or The Law. Members are required to conform to the Code and lifestyle. *"Those who do the will of God will come to know God."* Members must conform even before they have experienced God. The BCN Code expresses the basic demands of communalism. The way we live together defines our relationship with God.

- Requires love and concern for members.

- Makes fellowship possible.
- Seeks to enforce renunciation by clearly defining the boundaries separating the community from the slave culture.
- Seeks to protect the quality of life in the community—The Kingdom of God on earth.

The group is capable of divine enlightenment which comes with the actual experience of God. The group is both evangelical and revolutionary. Evangelical in that the group seeks to bring others into the fellowship because the community alone offers salvation and survival. Revolutionary in that the group seeks to bring the world into conformity with the will of God. The group labors for the redemption of the world and the building of a communal Pan African World Community.

The Practice of KUA takes the individual through seven distinct steps on the way to the climatic experience of God in Kugasana, which makes possible the healing when we become conduits for God's power with the laying on of hands.

- **Socialization** (through group participation and group encounter)
- **Preparing the Body** (through breathing, macrobiotic diet, Yoga, Tai Chi, African dance, etc.)
- **Preparing the Mind** (through re-experiencing experiences, psycho-drama enactments, psycho-history)
- **Spiritual Preparation** (through meditation, chaotic experiences, Seven KUA disciplines)
- **The Opening** (through rituals and sacraments, to let go giving control to God to break out of the prison house of rationality and attain a higher consciousness)
- **Kugasana Experience** (to experience God, to be possessed by the power of God)
- **The Laying on of Hands** (through the Seven KUA Affirmations; to become a conduit transmitting the power of God)

The Laying on of Hands

The Laying on of Hands is the basic healing ritual in the practice of KUA. When we have been opened to the experience of God, we are able to transmit the power and to heal and transform others.

We walk in the footsteps of Jesus by internalizing The Seven KUA Affirmations which take on a mystical power when combined with the Laying on of Hands reactivating and realigning the deepest levels of inner energy.

With spiritual preparation and faith that the power of God can act through us, we are able to transmit healing energy into the body of others by Laying on of Hands. The individual is opened, sensitized and enabled to internalize the Seven KUA Affirmations making them to foundation of faith and commitment, controlling and changing behavior.

The Seven KUA Affirmations
—The Laying on of Hands: Basic KUA Ritual of Healing—

The Seven KUA Affirmations are to be made at one time in a holy place with one or more KUA practitioners participating. The Affirmations are based upon key incidents in the life of Jesus as he went about the task of fulfilling his divine mission. A KUA Affirmation is spoken aloud while hands are laid upon each of the seven chakras-energy centers.

(First practitioner lays hands on each chakra. Second practitioner reads aloud the introduction statement, speaks the affirmation. First practitioner repeats).

THE FIRST KUA AFFIRMATION

(Root chakra—Muladhara)

Like every child growing up in the Black Nation Israel, Jesus was taught the Covenant, the Law, and the Prophets.

Like Jesus we accept the Covenant, the Law, and the Prophets as revelations of God binding upon His chosen people.

THE SECOND KUA AFFIRMATION—The Quest

(Navel chakra—Swadhisthana)

Jesus sought the experience of God when he left Nazareth and walked the dangerous Jericho Road to Jerusalem to be baptized in the Jordan River where he heard the voice of God declare him to be the Messiah and a dove lighting upon his shoulder symbolized the fact that he had received the Holy Spirit.

Like Jesus, we too, seek the experience of God. Kutafuta. Kutamungu. Kugasana. Kujitoa.

We Seek the Experience of God

Call and Response for Worship Service and Healing Ritual

Call: Kutafuta means that we have entered the sacred circle and we seek the experience of God.

Response: We open ourselves to receive the power of God.

Call: Kutamungu means that we can come upon God here where we are.

Response: If we seek, we will find.

Call: When we are open, our inner divinity can be touched by the Cosmic Power of God and **Kugasana** will come like a mystical explosion.

Response: The overwhelming power of God enters into us. The Creative Intelligence of God direst us. We become one with God and with our people everywhere.

Call: When our inner divinity comes into contact with the higher power out of which it was created, we are born again in the fullness of life.

Response: The sacred triangles, the mystical sacraments, and the disciplines of the Transforming Community open us to receive the power of God.

Call: In our surrender to God, **Kujitoa**, we have new strength for our earthly battles.

Response: We share a sacred trust with those who have gone before and with those who will come after. We are in total submission to the will of God, Kujitoa. Kutafuta. Kutamungu. Kugasana. Kujitoa

THE THIRD KUA AFFIRMATION—The Renunciation

(Solar plexus chakra—Manipura)

Following his baptism, Jesus went into the wilderness where he fasted and prayed for 40 days and 40 nights. He was tempted by Satan who offered him all of the glories of this world to turn his back upon God. Jesus rejected the temptations of Satan and renounced the slave culture by which Satan sought to tempt him.

Like Jesus, we too, renounce Satan and all his ways. We renounce the slave culture which tempts us with materialism, sensualism, and escapism. We place God first in our lives.

THE FOURTH KUA AFFIRMATION—The Power
(Heart chakra—Anahata)

Jesus with power of the Holy Spirit returned to Galilee and his reputation spread throughout the countryside. He taught in their synagogues and everyone praised him. He taught, preached, and healed.

Like Jesus, the power of the Holy Spirit is available to us. We, too, have the power to teach, preach, and heal.

In Matthew 21:22, it reads *"And if you have faith, everything you ask for in prayer, you will receive and everything that I do ye can do and more."*

THE FIFTH KUA AFFIRMATION—The Fellowship
(Throat chakra—Vishuddha)

He went up into the hills and summoned those he wanted. So, they came to him and he appointed twelve. They were to be his companions and to be sent out to preach with power and to cast out the devils and so he appointed twelve. (Mark 3:13-15)

His mother and brothers were standing outside and sent in a message. Jesus replied, "Who are my mother and my broths? And looking around at those sitting in a circle about him, he said, "Here are my mother and my brothers. Anyone who does the will of God, that person is my brother and sister and mother." (Mark 8:32-35)

Like Jesus, we recognize those associated with us in the task of building God's kingdom on earth as our family, and we have no other.

THE SIXTH KUA AFFIRMATION—The Betrayal

(Third eye chakra—Ajna)

In the Garden of Gethsemane, Jesus was betrayed by all of his disciples. We see how easily the disciples betrayed Jesus when they lost faith and began to doubt.

We will not betray the sacred community upon which we depend for both our salvation and our survival.

THE SEVENTH KUA AFFIRMATION—The Incarnation

(Crown chakra—Sahasrara)

According to the Gospel of Mark, Jesus was anointed Messiah at the time of his baptism. After their betrayal and flight, the disciples came back together for prayer and meditation. They became the Messianic Community when they were touched by the Holy Spirit at Pentecost.

Today, we accept this church as the Messianic Community with the mission and power which Jesus had during his lifetime. Everything Jesus did we can do.

APPENDIX B
Poetry by Jaramogi

"Eulogy for the Black Church"
The Church
Crumbling and empty.
Steeple titled,
Pointing crazily into the sky,
Stood among the rotting buildings
And stinking debris
Ministering in death
As it had in life.
Stating its theology
In mute elegance
With its crazy titled steeple
Pointing at the sky.

*

Smoke and fire
Spread an eerie pall over the urbanscape.
Furtive shadows
Darted in and out of the deserted buildings.
Screams and moans
Mingled with sounds of sporadic gunfire.
Dynamite blasting
And bulldozers pushing over vandalized buildings.
Five men dragged a
Screaming woman into the abandoned church.

*

The Ghetto was dying,
Raped and killed
To make room for white folks
Sneaking back from the suburbs
To retake the city from which they had fled.
The new stainless steel and glass
Air-conditioned white inner city
Would be closed to Blacks
Except for the beloved Black Mayor
Who had presided over the transition
Without inter-racial violence.
(No mean task!)
He would be allowed to remain
Until the Blacks were safely ensconced
In the new Black suburban Ghettoes.

*

Rev. Deauval was a preacher!
He made Old Mt. Zion
The most "powerful" Black Church in the Ghetto.
Of course, Rev. Deauval was a fine looking man too.
Tall and
Weighed at least 300 pounds.
Came north from New Orleans,
A Creole, they said.
He could "shout niggas by the acre."
"The best preacher

Memoir of a Black Christian Nationalist

Since John the Baptist
Pastored the First Baptist Church of Jerusalem."
Everybody called him, "The Candy Man!"
He really was a sweet thing,
And knew it too.
One Sunday morning
He was closing out his favorite sermon:
"He asked her for some,
And she told it all over town."
He was jumpin' up and down
With one hand cupped over his ear,
And he just up and died.
Turned sort of purple
And fell to the floor like a ton of lard.
Israel didn't mourn no more when Moses died
Than Old Mt. Zion mourned
The passing of the Candy Man.
Everybody who was anybody
Came to the Funeral.
The beloved Mayor made ingratiating remarks
About the Candy Man being "The Rock,"
Like Peter in the Bible.
When Sister Zelda fainted
While singing, "When I've Done the Best I Can,"
Old Mt. Zion went wild.
But Brother Twitty picked it right up
And kept it goin' for almost an hour.
Singing "Precious Lord, Take my Hand."
Finally, it was over.
Everyone had shouted out.

And there wasn't a tear left to shed.

*

The Black Weekly said
The Procession to the graveyard
Was "ten miles long,"
"With more than a hundred Cadillacs."
(The Jones men always had respected
the Candy Man).

*

The Ghetto never was the same
After the passing of the Candy Man.
And Old Mt. Zion just sort of fell apart.
Suddenly people noticed
That the Church was standing by itself
In the middle of a vacant block.
With only boarded up tenements in sight
Stores were all closed.
Except for some "Record Shops" selling weed
And a few Arab stores
Charging an arm-and-a-leg for a loaf of bread.
The "Candy Man" had mesmerized the Ghetto.
No one really noticed
That the world they lived in
Was falling apart;
Men out of work,
Crime,
Children selling dope,
And prostitution on every corner.

Memoir of a Black Christian Nationalist

Some said they saw it for the first time
On the way to the Graveyard
To lay the Candy Man to rest.
Not only the Candy Man was dead!
The Ghetto and Old Mt. Zion were dead.
Old Mother Tatum
Wiped a tear from her tired old eyes,
"Just like Jesus said on the Cross,"
She mumbled to no one in particular,
"It is finished,"
She was right,
The Black Church was dead!

On Being Black
When you are Black,
And poor
And oppressed
And unemployed,
Anger and frustration fill your mouth like vomit.
You, no longer know who you are
Or where you came from.
Only the stench and anguish of the slave ship,
And he indignity of the slave block,
With you naked
And ashamed,
Pawed and probed
By leering connoisseurs of Black flesh,
Seem real enough to be remembered.

*

Who are we?
Who am I?
I look about me
At Black brothers and sisters
Who look back
With furtive sullen eyes
Filled with rage and hostility.
And I know that they suffer as I suffer.
They are afraid as I am afraid.
They are confused as I am confused.
Somehow, we must break the chains
Which bind us to this oppressor.
His God.
His Flag.
His "Declaration of our inferiority."
He tells us that the ways of our ancestors
Were the ways of savages,
Forgetting the wanton barbarism
With which he raped our Motherland
To take us naked in chains
To build his nation.

*

We pour a libation to our ancestors,
And their spirits possess us.
We can hear the drums,
We dance the warriors' dance.
And we feel the thrill of battle.
The power of God enters into us

As we become one
In the Sacred Circle where God is.
Yes, we can learn to be as we were!
But only history can teach us
The rituals and disciplines
Used by our ancestors
To mold a "group"
To make men strong,
And women strong enough to send their lovers
Into battle with a song.

The Chosen
We are the Chosen of God,
The remnant,
Elected to survive
From the beginning of time.
We have come apart
Into the Transforming Community,
The Sacred Circle
Where the power of God is,
The Eternal Now!

*

The Apocalypse is upon us,
Everywhere things fall apart.
The cities to which we fled,
Leaving farms and friends
Are empty wastelands
With abandoned buildings
Boarded and crumbling

Hiding the Jones men
Who sell dreams in plastic bags for a "nickel."
Old men sprawl in alleyways
Drinking Twenty-Twenty and Wild Irish Rose.
Our sons roam the streets in packs
Preying the weak like Jackals,
While their sisters sell their bodies
On street corners,
Or give them away in dingy tinseled Disco Halls.
The machines have learned to run themselves
So the factories do not need us.
Soup Kitchens and Care packages from Europe
Sustain us.
If we were not the chosen of God,
The remnant elected to survive,
We would despair!

*

But let us sing no sad song to God
While we kneel trembling,
Waiting to do our master's bidding.
And let us sing no glad song
Until we break our chains
And standing tall and free
Bathed in the blood of our foes,
We can sing a glad song of struggle,
Sacrifice and freedom.
Then the beat of our hearts
Will be the drum of God
Resounding like thunder

Among the stars
In Galaxies far far away
And Kugasana, God will come.

Identification
Identification
The second Discipline
Touches the very core of my being
Calling me back to my ancestral roots
In Africa,
Where the first man was created
Black and beautiful
In a lush garden of plenty.
We were a "Chosen People,"
Favored above all people
Until we rebelled against God,
The cosmic power and creative intelligence
Out of which we have been created.
But we could not escape.
God remained incarnate within us.
Identification
Opens my eyes to the defilement
Of our enslavement
By a ruthless enemy
Who brutalizes and exploits
And declares us to be inferior.
I identify with my people everywhere.
Rejoicing in their triumphs,
And suffering their pain.
We are one.

I recoil from the brutal separation
Forced upon us.
The spiritual powers of my fathers
Engulf me.
The voice of the drums
Calls me back to the gods of my people,
And I join in their healing firelight dance
In the Sacred Circle beneath the stars.
Identification
Makes it possible for me to see the power of Jesus
Before he became the captive
Of the church
With its sterile white individualism
With its futile effort to wipe out
The African foundations of Christianity.
Identification with my brothers brought me back to God.

Renunciation

Renunciation
The first Discipline,
Demands conscious acts of confession,
Repentance, and penance.
I am strengthened for this task
By honest participation in the fellowship,
Rituals, encounters, and divine obligations
Of the "Group" to which I have been assigned.
Renunciation
Enables me to cast aside escapism in all its forms.
I renounce the acceptance of "Black Inferiority,"
Which I have been taught
By the operant conditioning of my white oppressor.
I renounce the futile dream of integration
Which wastes my energies
In vain efforts to create a "non-people."
I renounce the "slave culture,"
A sub-culture of the powerless,
Which has become for me a fantasyland
In which I dream away my life.
I renounce all of these weaknesses
Which block the building of a Black Community,
A counter-culture with power.
I carefully define boundaries and erect barriers
To separate me
From the evil insane world which I have renounced.

Transformation

Transformation.
The third Discipline
Involves the healing journey within
Whereby we free ourselves
From the protective shields and blocks
By which in isolation
We have sought to protect the ego
Which we have mistaken for our being.
We have lived lives of quiet desperation,
Locked in a prison house
Of loneliness
Afraid to bring the guilt
Of our repressed lives
Up into consciousness.
Deliberately
Choosing emptiness
To avoid vulnerability to pain,
We sought to anesthetize our emotions
So that we could neither love nor hate,
Nor feel.
We were closed away
In a shell of our own making.
Neither the sunrise nor the sunset
Could fill us with awe.
Neither the oceans,
The mountains,
A baby's laugh,
Nor a scream of pain
Could break through our defenses.

We were cut off from life
And experience.
We were the walking dead.
Transformation
Has shown us a light
At the end of a long tunnel.
We can change
If we but have the courage
To break down the walls of isolation
And "open" ourselves to the pain of KUA,
The pain of becoming what we already are.

Kutafuta
To Seek the Experience of God
(For the faithful, Kutafuta is a way of life. If one is always seeking, one will come upon God, Kutamungu).
Wretched and hopeless,
We are alone
And our aloneness is more painful
Than the misery which engulfs us.
We would cry out,
But we need a God to hear our cry,
To heal our pain,
To stop our wondering.
When we cry
The heavens are still,
And there is no answer.
The silence mocks us,
And we wonder
If God did speak,

Could we hear?
We are estranged
And alienated.
Perhaps God is not silent,
But we have no ears to hear.
We are locked in a prison house of self.
If we are to seek,
We must change,
Rejecting individualism,
Discarding false fronts,
Facing the repressions
Which conceal our guilt
And deaden our pain.
We must find the ancient disciplines
Used by Seekers in every generation.
The mysteries of the African Temples,
The miracles of Jesus, the Black Messiah,
The words of the prophet who spoke for God,
And the mystery of Pentecost
When the disciples of Jesus
Found Kugasana in the Upper Room.
These disciplines
Can open us
For the power of God
To enter into us,
To enlighten us,
And to transform us.
Kutafuta! Kutamungu! Kugasana! Kujitoa!

The Messiah

I am Black,
I am oppressed
And I seek to end my oppression.
I would strike out against it,
But I can neither understand it,
Nor face it.
Certainly, I must change
Both myself
And the society in which I live
But the nature of change evades me,
And all of my efforts have been in vain.

*

As we feel today,
So men felt 2,000 years ago
Until a child
Created out of the very substance of God
Discovered his inner divinity
And changed the world.
Who can foretell the birth of one
Who is to be anointed Messiah,
With power for the powerless,
Healing for the sick,
And liberation for those in chains?
"What I do ye can do and even more."
"The Kingdom of God is within you."
So every town and ghetto
Is Bethlehem.
And every child born of a Black Madonna

Is a new Messiah,
Only waiting to discover
His inner divinity.

The Covenant
The Narrow Gate to KUA, the Path of the Faithful
Many who seek
Do not find the narrow gate
Through which one must pass
To reach the path called KUA,
Said by ancient seers to lead to God.
The gate seems narrow
To one unaccustomed to the journey beyond reason.
The acceptance of a covenant
Before an encounter
Is like a contract with a shadow
Or a will-o-the wisp.
To give commitment and devotion
To God before one has felt the energy and power,
The intelligence,
Somehow seems strange if not insane
To say
I will serve Thee
And follow Thee
And love Thee
Before I know Thee.
Yet, why do we shrink back in fear?
It is not common practice
For millions of sane men
To make the commitment

To a structure, a building, a symbol
Without even the hope
Or the expectation
Of encounter.
To wager ones very salvation
Upon the report of another
Is even more strange
Than venturing out seeking
That which speaks to something deep within us.
So, weak and trembling,
We seek to enter the narrow gate
Through which we must pass
To find the Path called KUA
Which ancient seers and gurus followed
When they sought
The Experience of God.
Kutafuta! Kutamungu! Kugasana! Kujitoa!

Kujitoa
Surrender
We confess our sins, Kukiri.
We cry out in pain,
Until we find KUA,
The path of the faithful,
And spirit, mind, and body become one.
We step into the sacred circle, Duara,
A place dedicated to God
Where the energy of God can enter into us.
And we are in the Motherland
Standing upon earth hollowed by our fathers' blood.

We have returned to the ancient source of all things.
We upon ourselves to them, Wazi,
And accept the covenant of Abraham, Isaac, and Jacob.
We have been created out of the very substance of God
But our divine inner nature is concealed,
Until touched by the Cosmic Power of God Transcendent,
Then Kugasana comes like a mystical explosion,
Ugana Shango Kibwa.
We surrender ourselves, Kujitoa.
The overwhelming power of God enters into us.
The creative intelligence of God directs us.
We become one with God
And with our people everywhere.
Kutamungu has brought us to life.
The Sacred Triangles,
The mystical Sacraments,
The disciplines of the Transforming Community
Bind us together.
In our surrender to God, Kujitoa,
We have new strength for our earthly battles, Vita.
The commitment,
The skills,
The power,
And the will to dedicate our lives
To God and to each other.
We share a sacred trust
With those who have gone before
And those who will come after.
We are in total submission to the will of God.
Kujitoa.

We Will Survive

We have lived in a dream world
Of fantasy and "let's pretend,"
Blind to the ugly reality
Which was all about us
And within us,
And to the dangers
Which threatened to engulf and destroy us.
But like a mighty giant
Awakening from a deep sleep,
We stretch, rub the sleep from our eyes,
Look at the world
And what it has done to us
And cry out in rage!

*

We are not afraid.
Without jobs, money, or skills,
We will survive.
The anguish of our suffering
Created
Out of the very substance of God
We have come together
In the "Transforming Community"
Where the power of God is.
We labor in love
And communal fellowship
To build a promised land.
We are destined to inherit the earth.
So stand tall.

Appendix B

Be conscious of the divinity within you.
Be proud of what we were.
Be proud of what we are
And of what we can become.
Thank God
Who made us
The most beautiful people,
The most powerful of people,
And the best of people.
Black is beautiful.
Black is strong.
Black is good.
The secret of our beauty,
Strength,
And goodness
Lies in our loyalty
And total submission
To the will of God.
Kujitoa.
We will survive!

The Baptism of Fire

Spiritual Matters
Are never simple, clear, and plain
To be understood and accepted
Without pain, torment
And inner doubts.
It is as though
We are dying in the act of being born
Being consumed
In the fires of creating.
As John the Baptist said of Jesus,
"He who comes after me
Will baptize you with fire and the Holy Spirit."
Did the disciples
Feel the pain and ecstasy
Of their fiery baptism
As they walked with Jesus
By the Sea of Galilee
And asked among themselves,
What does he mean?
Or when at night
They tossed and turned.
The act of being changed,
Of moving
Toward the experience of God
Is to be seared
By the white-hot flame of pure being,
The energy of God.
And to feel God seeking to possess us,
Breaking through the barriers of consciousness,

Of ego,
Of body/mind blocks.
To contact the consuming inner fire
Of God incarnate.
This is the mystical transforming explosion
When nothing is real
But the power and creative intelligence of God,
The fiery baptism
When God comes,
Kugasana!
The world is corrupt
And we are a part of the corruption.
Unless we can redeem it,
The consuming fire of God's anger
Will come,
And the world will be destroyed.
We would like to disentangle ourselves,
To go apart
Into the sanctuary
Of a Transforming Community
Where God could protect us.
But when we try to turn away
We realize
That the corrupt world is also in us.
And wherever we to
We take the corruption with us.
Only the baptism of fire can cleanse us!
Let the fire come quickly
We pray.
Only the experience of God

Can save us!
Kugasana!
The science of KUA
Helps us open ourselves to God.
We feel cosmic energy flood our being.
We close our eyes,
And we can hear the drums of God.
We hear the soft wind in veldt grass
And a far off flute
With a tune too sweet to bear.
We are at peace.
There is nothing which we must do,
Or must not do.
Nothing which we must think,
Or not think.
We follow the prompting of the Holy Spirit
Like the disciples at Pentecost
When they spoke in strange tongues
And a mighty wind filled the room
Where they were,
And tongues of fire rested over each head.
A fiery baptism,
Where the transforming community was born,
And the corruption of the world,
Was consumed by fire.
The Kingdom of God has come!
We are in the Kingdom.
The Kingdom is within us.
And we wait patiently for its' coming.
Kutafuta! Kutamungu! Kugasana! Kujitoa!

APPENDIX C
BCN Covenant

Declaring ourselves to be God's chosen people, created in His image, the living remnant of the lost Black Nation, Israel, we come together as brothers and sisters in the Black Christian Nationalist Movement. We are Disciples of the Black Messiah, Jesus of Nazareth, who by his life, and by his death upon the cross, teaches us that nothing is more sacred than the liberation of Black people.

We covenant together and pledge our total commitment to the task of rebuilding a Black Nation with power here on earth. We will do whatever is necessary to achieve self-determination for Black people. We will fight the injustice, oppression, and exploitation of all Black people. As members of the Black Nation, we are bound together in an inseparable sacred brotherhood. To the service of this sacred brotherhood, we pledge our lives.

APPENDIX D
BCN Statement of Faith

The myth of creation holds that in the beginning God created the first man, Adam, a Black man, and placed him in a beautiful garden located somewhere in Africa. Adam was expelled from the Garden of Eden because of the sin of individualism (egocentrism). He revolted against God.

In Africa, the Black man developed the world's first great civilization with religion, science, philosophy and a knowledge of the mysteries. Seeking to expiate the sin of individualism for which he had been expelled from the Garden of Eden, the Black man developed a communal way of life in which each individual merged his life into the life of the group and the life of the group became more important than his own.

God recognized the Black man's repentance and made his First Covenant with the Black Patriarch, Abraham, declaring the Black Nation Israel to be His chosen people, and bestowing upon them a Promised Land flowing with milk and honey. Whenever the Black Nation sinned and returned to individualism, God punished them and placed them in bondage first to their cousins, and then to the white heathens and barbarians.

The period of the First Covenant drew to a close with the failure of Jesus, the Black Messiah, to liberate Israel from white oppression, the fall of Jerusalem, and the Diaspora (the scattering of Black people throughout the world) which climaxed in the hoors and brutality of the African slave trade.

The Second Covenant (the ascendency of the Black Man) was announced by Marcus Garvey and began with the call of the Black Christian Nationalist Church to Black people everywhere to join in a worldwide religious struggle for Black Liberation.

We share the faith of Jesus of Nazareth. We embody the revolutionary power of God revealed in Jesus and his struggle to liberate Black people from white oppression. We realize that the Second Covenant may be one of violence, suffering, and sacrifice because Black people may be called upon to fight their oppressors in a final struggle for survival (the Battle of Armageddon). The white man's cruel power establishment is crumbling and in his frantic last hours, he may attempt our genocide. He will fail because BCN is bringing

Black people together and organizing for survival. We are the power of God unto salvation. This will soon be revealed to the world by the power of the Holy Spirit manifest in us. The Messiah for whom Israel waited is now incarnate in BCN. God testifies for us through the works that we do.

The Apostolic power bestowed upon the disciples by Jesus, claimed by the Holy Catholic Church (mediated through the sacraments) is now the sacred possession of BCN because we alone in this day understand and continue the revolutionary ministry of Jesus. The power to prophesy, to heal, and to forgive sins is being bestowed upon us daily by the Holy Spirit. We reject the Protestant heresy of "individualistic salvation" attainable without the mediation of the church because we know that the Holy Spirit is a group-experience unattainable by the individual. We are apocalyptic, apostolic, Pentecostal, and messianic. We are the instrument of God for the liberation of Black people. We teach the mysteries of the Divine Triangle, the Baptism of the Holy Spirit, the spiritual psychological conversion of the group process, and the revolutionary concept of positive righteousness.

We prepare for the Third Covenant, God's restoration of the Black man and woman to rule over all the nations of the world in power and righteousness forever and ever.

APPENDIX E
BCN Code

The BCN Code is a simplified basic statement of the day-to-day behavioral requirements for BCN membership as outlined in the BCN Creed, Program, Position, and Teachings, and explained in The Black Messiah and Black Christian Nationalism. It presupposes total commitment to the liberation of Black people, the religious faith that nothing is more sacred than the liberation of Black people, and the philosophical conviction that both right and wrong, and good and evil must be judged only in terms of whether or not any particular act contributes to the liberation struggle of Black people. All members of BCN are bound by the BCN Code, and disciplinary action (probation, suspension, or expulsion) will be taken whenever an infraction occurs.

Section I—Security

Any action which threatens the security of the Black Nation is forbidden. The breaking of the laws of the country in which we reside through anger, frustration, or unauthorized non-programmatic confrontation threaten the security of the Black Nation and are forbidden. The use, possession or sale of illegal drugs is expressly forbidden.

Article I—All members of BCN are required to report anything that is detrimental to the Nation, in or out of a Nation institution.

Article II—All members of the Nation are required to refrain from the use of drugs.

Article III—All members of BCN are required to report all gossip to the proper authority (group leader or Maccabee-security branch).

Article IV—There will be no loitering in front of any BCN institution.

Article V—The property of the Nation is sacred and valuable. It is the duty of every member to take care of it and protect it.

Section II—Subversion

Any action designed to weaken the stability of the Nation from within is forbidden. Subversive unauthorized gatherings or meetings, and the dissemination of propaganda or gossip unfavorable to BCN in any form whatsoever is forbidden.

Article I—All members of BCN are required to obey all regulations, codes, laws, morals and ethics as determined by the BCN National Chairman.

Article II—All counter-revolutionary activities and revision is against BCN Security Policy.

Article III—All members of BCN are required to be constantly on the alert to prevent infiltration by the enemy.

Article IV—Members of BCN are required to obey and follow all instructions from the BCN Chain of Command.

Article V—All members of BCN are required to be truthful and honest with the Nation and not conceal or distort the truth.

Article VI—No member is allowed membership while still participating in another organization whose program or time requirements prevent total commitment to BCN.

Article VII—No member of BCN is permitted to make an official statement without first having it cleared by the National Chairman.

Article VIII—Association with persons who have been expelled from the Nation is forbidden.

Section III—Moral and Ethics

Any action which tends to weaken the basic family structure of the Nation is forbidden. (A man and a woman who live together as man and wife and represent themselves to the Nation as man and wife are in the eyes of the Nation, in fact, man and wife, and are required to accept all the normal responsibilities of marriage). Any action which tends to disrupt a family or hold the BCN family structure up to ridicule either by infidelity to one's own mate or by encroaching upon the sanctity of the marriage of another, is forbidden. Promiscuity is expressly forbidden whether or not the individuals involved are married. The spreading of venereal disease within the Nation is considered a crime. Members are required to report cases of venereal disease immediately and to present satisfactory evidence of competent medical treatment.

All children and young people in the Nation are considered wards of the Nation and under its protection. The sexual exploitation of children and young people either by adults or by other children and young people is expressly forbidden. The Alkebu-lan Oath which is a part of the BCN Wedding Ceremony clearly expresses the BCN response to the sexual exploitation of Sisters in any manner whatsoever.

Article I—All members of BCN are required to control personal feelings when dealing with anything organizational. Continuous infractions will call for disciplinary actions.

Article II—All parents are accountable for their children's behavior, health, discipline, cleanliness, and education.

Article III—Members must make every effort to maintain good health and a bi-yearly physical examination is required.

Article IV—Excessive drinking is prohibited.

Article V—Actions or words indicating disrespect for anyone in a leadership position will be interpreted as counter-revolutionary and are expressly prohibited.

Article VI—All members of BCN are required to respect all African people because we are struggling to free Black people all over the world.

Section IV—Participation and Study

BCN requires that all members participate fully in its program (Liberation Triangle) and seriously prepare for leadership through systematic study and regular training group attendance. Members who fail to meet these basic requirements will be disciplined.

Article I—Membership in BCN is open to all Black people who are willing to commit themselves to the liberation struggle of Black people.

Article II—All members of BCN must study BCN Philosophy diligently and strive unceasingly to raise the level of their understanding in all aspects of the liberation struggle.

Article III—All members of BCN are required to be active in a cadre or group in order to experience the group process.

Article IV—All members of BCN are required to faithfully carry out BCN Policy and energetically fulfill the tasks assigned to them.

Article V—All members of BCN are required to place the interests of the Nation above their own and in the event of any conflict between the two submerge individualism in the interest of the Nation.

Article VI—All members of BCN are required to set a good example for Black people all over the world in everything they do.

Article VII—All members of BCN are required to work constantly to raise their productive skills and professional abilities.

Article VIII—All members of BCN are required to be present at all meetings and classes to which they have been assigned unless properly excused.

Article IX—Members of BCN are required to carry the BCN Position, Program, and Teaches to all Black people and to evidence the BCN life style at all times.

Article X—It is every working member's duty to pay Kodi—taxation to build a Black Nation.

Article XI—It is the duty of every adult member to raise his understanding of traditional African religious beliefs and to teach them to their children.

Article XII—Kazi, communal work, is an essential part of BCN membership, and members are required to participate regularly.

Article XIII—All members of BCN are required to Kusanya Watu (recruit) prospective members.

Article XIV—All members of BCN are required to practice criticism and self-criticism by utilizing the group process. Expose shortcomings and mistakes in work and struggle to overcome and correct them.

Article XV—All members of BCN are required to be neat and clean.

Article XVI—All members of BCN are required to be properly uniformed when required.

Article XVII—All members of BCN are required to obey BCN curfews.

BCN College Cadre Code

The College Cadre is specifically designed for College Cadre members and is intended to supplement sections of the BCN Code (Laws for the Black Nation) and not to replace them. It seeks to clarify and interpret the BCN Code recognizing the unique problems created by the transitory and artificial life of the American College campus for young adults who have had little opportunity to act as responsible adults nor to consider education seriously as preparation for participation in the Black man's liberation struggle.

Section I

All members are required to pursue a course of study designed to prepare them for more effective participation in the Black Liberation Struggle as defined by BCN and are expected to maintain a 3.0 grade point average.

Article I—Cadre members ought to request special help in selecting a relevant course of study from the National Office.

Article II—All cadres must arrange their activities, classes, and assignments in such a manner as to leave ample time for study. Special consideration must be given to the need for extra study time for examinations and term papers.

Article III—A cadre leader must consider an individual member's total workload including classes and slave jobs necessary for economic survival in making assignments.

Article IV—Only Friday orientation, Saturday Kazi, and Sunday Karamu Festival (when held) are required of all members unless excused specifically by the cadre leader.

Section II

Cadre members may engage in a normal campus social life, dating both in and out of the cadre, and attending campus activities. Insofar as Section III of the BCN Code is not transgressed, members and their dates may attend the movies and eat dinner out in town. (Bars and off campus slave culture parties remain off limits).

Section III

All other Sections of the BCN Code pertaining to security, subversion, morals and ethics, participation and study remain unchanged for College Cadre members except insofar as they are specifically clarified in the preceding Sections of the College Cadre Code for Black Christian Nationalists.

APPENDIX F
BCN Program

I. The Black Church must seriously work for the liberation of Black people through the realization of concrete and attainable goals here on earth as defined by the Black Christian Nationalist Movement.

II. BCN understands the vicious power reality of the white man's imperialistic, capitalistic and individualistic society, and fights to free Black men from it by giving a revolutionary programmatic structure and direction to the Black Church by re-affirming the African origins of Christianity and the historic Blackness of the biblical Nation Israel and the Black Messiah, Jesus, as the basis of our struggle for African Redemption and the Liberation of Black people everywhere.

III. Realizing that power resides in institutions and not in individuals, BCN works to establish and develop counter institutions essential to a Pan-African Communal Black Society.

a. BCN works to build a revolutionary Black Church with a new Black Theology to serve the interests of Black people.

b. BCN works to build new Black schools which can re-affirm the Black man's original African identity, build a new commitment to African communal living, and teach the skills necessary for life in a highly technical industrial society.

c. BCN works to build a complex of urban and rural communes within which Black people can receive many of the advantages of African communal living in the satisfaction of everyday needs.

d. BCN works to create and implement a new Black economics which will enable many Black people to labor within a communal environment which places top priority upon service to the Black community.

e. BCN works to create a new independent Black political structure capable of focusing maximum political power in support of the interests of the Black community as defined by BCN.

f. BCN works to establish Black hospitals and social agencies to serve the Black community.

g. BCN works to establish a Pan-African communications network uniting African people and Black Liberation movements throughout the world.

h. BCN words to support separatist Black liberation movements everywhere.

i. BCN works for African Redemption (the liberation, unification, and industrialization of our Motherland Africa) as the cornerstone of the BCN position.

j. Even as we work to build a world-wide institutional base for Pan-Africanism, we commit our lives and our resources to defend and protect Black communities and institutions functioning within the framework of the BCN position.

APPENDIX G
BCN Teaches

1. Nothing is more sacred than the liberation of Black people.
2. The dream of "integration" reflects our acceptance of the myth of Black inferiority, and serves as the basis for our continuing enslavement.
3. Even within the framework of a correct analysis, philosophy, and program projection, it is impossible to build an effective organization without loyalty, discipline, and a clearly defined chain of command.
4. Individualism is a beast within each of us. We must fight the beast within as well as the beast without.
5. Black people are separate in every way and we must use our separateness as a basis for achieving power.
6. Black people had a rich and glorious history and culture long before the white man emerged from the caves.
7. The spirituality of African people encompasses the totality of life. Politics and economics are sacred because they offer programmatic mechanisms for our struggle against white oppression.
8. Properly interpreted, the Bible is a history of God's relationship with the African Nation, Israel, and the Black Messiah, Jesus. Without a correct BCN interpretation, the Bible has served to confuse and enslave a powerless Black people who have waited in vain for deliverance here on earth, and for transportation to a mythical heaven in the sky after death.
9. The "Latter Days" foretold by the Prophets ended almost 2,000 years ago. The end was climaxed by the fall of Jerusalem, and the Fort of Masada, and the dispersion of the Black Nation Israel throughout the world. The prophecies of the Bible cannot be applied literally to the problems and realities of today. Biblical prophecy voiced the will of God for the African Nation Israel at a particular time and place.
    a. Only the ignorant wait for the fulfillment of the prophecies addressed to a past which is dead and finished.
    b. BCN is the living prophetic voice of God for African people in this day, and

our prophecies will come to past when Black people totally commit their lives to the struggle against white oppression.

10. God has historically chosen to work through groups and nations rather than through individuals. As shown in the Bible, the God of the Black Nation works through the power of the group experience to transform individuals and to bring into being a communal Black Nation.

APPENDIX H
BCN Position

I. We are an African people and the redemption of Africa is the cornerstone of the BCN Position.
   a. Our Motherland was raped, many of our brothers and sisters were kidnapped, brutalized, and dispersed throughout the world.
   b. All African people have been declared inferior by our enemy, the white man.

II. Our total existence for the past 400 years has been one of enslavement. We have been used in the building of white institutions which serve the interests of our white enemy and perpetuate our enslavement.

III. Recognizing that these conditions have constituted a process which has rendered us powerless and psychologically sick, we struggle for the liberation of Black people:
   a. by changing the minds of Black people from individualism to communalism, utilizing the BCN group process;
   b. by providing support for African freedom movements, and financial and technical existence for African economic development;
   c. by developing powerful counter-institutions serving the interests of Black people and resulting in a technological industrial African communal society.

APPENDIX I
BCN Goals at Basic Training Levels

We Share a Common Past
1. Four hundred years of enslavement
2. Powerlessness
3. Oppression
4. Acceptance of declaration of Black inferiority
5. Development of a slave culture of fantasy, escapism, identification, materialism and individualism

STG (Support Training Group) Level I
1. I believe that BCN is the Answer to the Black man's problems.
2. I will attend services, whenever possible and support all special events and programs. I will support the Black Slate and all political programs supported by BCN.
3. Realizing that my participation in BCN is not total, I am willing to contribute sacrificially each week.

STG (Support Training Group) Level II
1. I believe that BCN offers the only answer to the Black man's problems, and that BCN offers the only sound programmatic approach to Black liberation.
2. Although at this time, I am not able to give total commitment to BCN, I am willing to commit my skills to the Black Nation. I will contribute regularly to finance the Black Nation. I will support, work, and organize special affairs for fund raising and publicity for Black political power through the Black Slate. I am willing to run and take office when asked by BCN.
3. I will give total support to those brothers and sisters in Advanced Training Group (ATG) and at cadre level because I understand that they have given total commitment to the liberation struggle of Black people.
4. I will learn and know the basics of BCN Theology, program and philosophy. I understand the need for communal living as the only way of life for Black people.

BTG (Basic Training Group) Level III

1. I believe that there is nothing more important than the liberation of Black people and that BCN offers the only sound programmatic approach to Black liberation.
2. The slave culture has rendered me incapable of seriously participating in the liberation struggle unless I can first be changed, discarding individualism, my slave culture life style, and my acceptance of the white man's declaration of Black inferiority.
3. I realize that I must choose between the BCN world of liberation and the world of slavery. I know that I cannot change myself without the BCN group process and I voluntarily seek to subordinate myself to the group which I am assigned for a period of sixteen weeks of basic training using the objective criteria of my participation in the Liberation Triangle to determine whether or not I am capable of change.

ATG (Advanced Training Group) Level IV

1. Having completed my basic training, I realize that I have only begun the process of change. I still need the support of the group and the objective criteria of the Liberation Triangle to test my seriousness.
2. I feel a growing inner sense of commitment to BCN as the instrument by which Black people are to be liberated and a growing awareness of the demands which total commitment will make upon my life.
3. I am willing to give total commitment to BCN as the only existing instrument by which Black people are to be liberated and a growing awareness of the powerless condition we are now living in. I will accept assignment to an expansion cadre or to any other leadership position to which the Black Nation may call me, seriously undertaking such additional training as may be necessary.

Expansion Cadre (Leadership Level) Level V

I give total commitment to BCN as the instrument by which Black people are to be liberated. I will accept any sacrifice I may be called upon to make. I expect to be held accountable for all of my actions and will accept any disciplinary action the proper authority in the chain of command may take if my actions in any way indicated neglect of duty, insubordination, individualism, revisionism or a reversion to slave culture behavior. I expect disciplinary action at this leadership level to be more swift and harsher than it would be at a lower level because failure at this level endangers BCN and the liberation of Black people.

APPENDIX J
BCN Basic Training Pledge

Our forefathers were stolen from our Motherland, Africa, and brought to the land of our enemy in chains and brutally forced to build a nation for our oppressor. For 400 years, Black people have endured a wretched condition of enslavement and powerlessness. We have been exploited and brutalized. The enemy who has determined the conditions of our existence has destroyed our unity as a people, robbed us of our cultural heritage and the knowledge of our glorious past. Finally, he has succeeded in convincing us of our own inferiority.

Today, our labor is no longer needed by our enemy who has created a highly developed system of industrial automation and cybernation, eliminating the need for at least 80% of his present labor supply. (Yette) Increasing unemployment, the reduction of public relief, forced sterilization of Black women, police state brutality, and prisons filled to overflowing with Black men, mark the first visible signs of our oppressor's planned genocide for Black people.

The absurdity of Negro churches and organizations seeking to program for Black liberation in terms of integration with our enemy is now obvious. The dream of integrating perpetuates our powerlessness and is the mechanism of our continued enslavement. The survival of Black people in America depends upon the BCN Ten Year program of expansion. Organizing for power and liberation. BCN is the only answer. Our choice is simple. Support the BCN Program or die!

Our future does not depend upon the white man but upon what we do now to organize for liberation. We realize that 400 years of enslavement and powerlessness has rendered us psychologically sick. We are products of a slave culture. Our minds have been shaped by the slave culture into which our oppressor has forced us. Identification with the enemy, individualism, materialism, patterns of irresponsibility, sensualism, and the blind rage of frustration, characterize our everyday behavior. BCN seeks to structure a new life style and time rituals. This is the Group Process in which each member is required to participate because it is the instrument by which we can change each other and prepare Black brothers and sisters for leadership in a revolutionary struggle for Black liberation.

As a new member, you are required to participate in a Basic Training Group (BTG) and experience the revolutionary Group Process for a period of at least 16 weeks before being given an African name and being promoted to an Advanced Training Group (ATG). If any member fails to consistently move toward the new BCN lifestyle as evidenced by the following tests of change even after completing Basic Training), he will be recycled into a Decision Group (DTG) where he can be given special assistance.

References

Books

Cleage, Albert. BCN Souvenir Booklet 1975.

Cleage, Albert. BCN Souvenir Booklet 1987.

Dudley, Dean. 1925. *History of the First Council of Nice: A World's Christian Convention A.D. 325 with a Life of Constantine.* EWorld Inc.

Emmons, Robert A. 2000. "Is Spirituality an Intelligence?" *The International Journal for the Psychology of Religion* 10: 27–34.

Kushi, Michio. 1979. *The Book of Do-In: Exercise for Physical and Spiritual Development.* Japan Publications.

Lidell, Lucy, Narayani, and Giris Rabinovitch. 1988. *The Sivananda Companion to Yoga.* Simon and Schuster.

McIntosh, Shelley. 2001. *Genesis II: The Re-Creation of Black People.* Africa World Press.

McIntosh, Shelley. 2005. *Mtoto House: Vision to Victory: Raising African American Children Communally.* Hamilton Books.

Schonfield, Hugh J. 1964. *The Passover Plot.* Hugh and Helene Schonfield World Service Trust.

Schonfield, Hugh J. 1974. *The Jesus Party.* Macmillan.

Schonfield, Hugh J. 1975. *For Christ's Sake: A Discussion of the Jesus Enigma.* London: Macdonald & Jane's.

Schonfield, Hugh J. 1984. *The Essene Odyssey: The Mystery of the True Teacher and the Essene Impact on the Shaping of Human Destiny.*

Schonfield, Hugh J. 1991. *The Pentecost Revolution: The Story of the Jesus Party in Israel, AD 36–66.* MacDonald's and Jane's.

Tamarkin, Noah. 2020. *Genetic Afterlives: Black Jewish Indigeneity in South Africa.* Durham, North Carolina: Duke University Press.

Willhelm, Sidney. 1993. *Who Needs the Negro?* CB Pub & Design.

Yette, Samuel F. 1996. *The Choice: The Issue of Black Survival in America.* Cottage Books.

Websites

Forbes, Natalie Wexler (https://www.forbes.com/sites/nataliewexler)

Forgotten Books—The Apocrypha Hidden Books of the Bible (forgottenbooks.org)

Pew Research Center (www.pewresearch.org).

USA Facts, 2019 Annual Report (https://annualreport.usafacts.org).

Who Were the Pharisees? Bible Definition and Meaning (biblestudytools.com)

About the Author

SHELLEY MCINTOSH HELD POSITIONS IN HIGHER EDUCATION, PUBLIC school administration, and regional educational service agency. She is the founder, chief education officer, and chief executive officer of Child Focused Consulting Company, LLC, which provides instructors for reading intervention and science instruction. *Memoir of a Black Christian Nationalist: Seeds of Liberation* is her fifth book. She is also the author of *Genesis II: The Re-Creation of Black People, Mtoto House: Vision to Victory-Raising African American Children Communally, A Principal's Tale: Life in 31 Days,* and *A Principal's Tale: A Self-Determined Leader.* Her focus is leadership and literacy. She holds bachelor of science, master of education, and doctoral degrees in curriculum and instruction and is certified in teaching and school administration. Shelley lives in Michigan where her daughter, son, and grandsons reside.

shelleymcintosh.com

www.ingramcontent.com/pod-product-compliance
Lightning Source LLC
Chambersburg PA
CBHW081344070526
44578CB00005B/724